Mirror, Mirror
In the Geography of the Head

Sam Smith

erbacce-press
Liverpool UK

erbacce-press publications Liverpool UK 2022

erbacce-press.com
ISBN: 978-1-912455-30-0

acknowledgements

Some of these poems have appeared individually, and in groups, in the following publications:

Aireings, And What of Tomorrow?, Apostrophe, ASWELLas, The Avon Literary Intelligencer, Axion, Borderlines, Braquemard, Brass Butterfly, The Brobdingnagian Times (Ireland), *Bubble, Chronicles of Disorder, Cleopatra* (Italy), *The Coffee House, Connections, Creative Tales, Doors, Eco Runes, End of Millennium, Envoi, Fire, First Time, The Frogmore Papers, Front Cover* (Ireland), *Headlock, Hybrid, International Writers Association* (USA), *Ixion* (www), *The Kerouac Connection, Kickin' & Screamin', Lines Review, Links, Linkway, the magazine, Manchester Poetry, Memes, Micropress Oz* (Australia), *Moonstone, Never Bury Poetry, New Hope International, The New Writer, Nineties Poetry, Northwords, Ocular, Odyssey, Orbis, Ore, Paladin, Parasol Post, Parnassus* (India), *Pennine Platform, Poetry Monthly, Poetry Nottingham, Poetry Now, Printed matter* (Japan), *Pulsar, Purple Patch, Quantum Leap, The Rialto, River KingPoetry Supplement* (USA), *roundyhouse, Rustic Rub, Smile, Smiths Knoll, SODEM, Sol, Songs, Staple, Lo Straniero* (Italy), *Terrible Work, 3x4, TOPS, Tremblestone, Uncompromising Positions, Understanding, Unicorn, Voice & Verse, Voyage, Weyfarers. White Rose, Wire* and *Writers Viewpoint.*

Index

Present & Future 101

Now, Here

In the asylum on a winter's night
pale crickets cheep
among the heating pipes.

Now is the slow time of stones,
their hot creation and cold erosion,
where a beetle can plod on
indiscreetly
through dry leaf litter
under dry cracking trees.

Along squeaking asylum corridors
endlessly curving,
in boxed ceiling conduits,
among looped, colour-coded cables,
unseen crickets cheep.

The echoes are quick and sibilant,
without focus.

As if here there wasn't,
already,
confusion enough.

Self-Contained

Distantly the sound comes
through doors and echoing up walls
a man giving a bark like a big dog.
Phlegm bubbles and the bark rasps out
through a throat already inflamed.
a mind caught up on the petulant production
of phlegm and the explosion of cough,

A bent man in disorganised clothes
begs cigarettes in the entrance foyer.
A dribbling woman too drips her fingertips
on passing sleeves. Along the corridor,
singing and marching, comes a thin woman.
And goes. Another arrives in a rush and
sobbing histrionically.
She is ignored
by shutdown selves in shop and canteen.

Another mind on another ward
has magnified or misremembered her pain
and she yelps - yow yow yow yow - starting
even at the prospect of being moved. She
sounds like a seagull calling. Also distantly.

To Be Right, To Do Right

He was a big man, no neck.
Roaring
        he began to kick out the ward windows.
I grabbed him away, shouted his name into his face,
asked him what he thought he was doing.

All over him muscles pulled one against the other.
"I'm a good man Sam." he said, "Whole of my life
 I have done as God and the voices told me."

Then he let us inject him.

The Nursing Assistant's Dream

I'm at work
have got John Clare
by the thin soft part above the elbow
am guiding him back indoors
(institutionalised depressives come slow
  irritatingly slow, but easy)
This scruffy old man
- associations of incontinence
  unshaken dribbles -
is due a bath
I take another sniff
No. This old man, pink and round,
has been crawling through undergrowth again
smells of black earth and blue skies

Palmistry

On the pill round,
tapping tablets from small plastic pots
into pink palms,
I notice, worriedly,
how many have the same single simian line
cutting across their pink palm
as I.
'...denotes strong inner tensions...'
This job does not come easy:
I know I am not immune, exempt
from these illnesses, that only a feather's stretch
stops me being the one
passively holding out my hand.

Speech! Speech!

Brains smoothed,
minds empty,
these old people continue to use
patterns of speech
- hectoring, matey,
  wheedling, sarcastic
that they used when
they were thought to know
what they were talking about.
Here though
they repeat and repeat
the same remarks;
and in this context of shined floors
and the reek of incontinence
none of it makes sense.

John Clare

I have seen men sat on wards
crouching over their pockets' contents,
organising an identity around
bottle tops, tobacco wrappers, an important form.
I have seen men on wards with,
in their pockets,
whole toilet rolls, flattened,
and scribbled over
end to end in slanted code.
Corners of magazines,
the porous insides of packages,
have been invested with tiny calligraphy
and words so profound that,
taken all together,
they become banal.
I have sat with men on wards
and we have looked out together
through small squared panes
at grounds enclosed by trees,
a view curtailed by summer haze.
I have sat with men
in their massive suicidal silence,
and to mark the passing of my time
I have talked,
pointing out a spotted flycatcher,
"Look, tied by elastic to its perch."
Fluttering out and back again.
"See.
  Out and back again."
"See.
Out and back again."

Sounds Of Time Passing

Words,
pieces of grit
fingerflicked
into the glass bowl
of the skull

ping
and zing
with nothing soft
to absorb
or deflect
their trajectories.

Time
here is
without walls,
without boundaries.
In the corridors
a tobacco economy;
begged cigarettes
pegging out the hours.

Smalltalk (1)

My job once was to sit with men and women who were
intent on suicide. My priority
was to physically stop them harming themselves
- with broken glass or belts or misappropriated medicines.
My secondary task was to try to talk them out of
their negative and self-destructive attitudes
while avoiding the negative addition of guilts.
(Think how your family will miss you.)
I became ingenious in my devising of innocent reasons
for anyone to stay alive:
the prospect of more rainbows for instance. But,
if any of those men and women did change their minds,
they changed their own minds.
I simply occupied their time and mine.

Time Flies

The human brain can distinguish movement
to seven millionths of a single second.

Glance now to the corner of the eye.

My
how time flies
when I'm standing by
how time stands still
when I'm within arm's reach
of someone hectically psychotic.

Projection

Simpled mind fastens
>here
onto one particle
of our culture,
of our taken for granted ordinary
>everyday lives
and then repeats it, and repeats it,
>"Yes please. Thank you very much.
>Please thank you. Very much please.
>Thank you yes. Please. Yes very much.
>Thank you.   Thank you.
>Thank you."

Mirror, Mirror On The Ward...

>Those labelled mad are most frightening
>>because
>they reflect back at us
>aspects of ourselves
>>magnified
>that don't make sense,
>that make an awful sense.
>A mind caught up on one
>hiccupping anxiety of our time,
>>fear visible,
>>adrenalin in every muscle,
>>the contagious,
>>glancing about terror
>>of a trapped bird.

A Watcher

A watcher of other people
sleep I have sat all night
willing my mind awake. Now,
crosseyed with tiredness,
I open curtains and behold
planet Earth tilt into dawn,
see sunlight slide pink
to golden up under
ribbed blue clouds.

(Cycling to work last evening
I watched a kestrel hover
before a round white moon,
long set.)

Going home I pedal over
        an old railway bridge.
Below its iron panels
        three jackdaws use
a dead ash's knobbled branches
        as vantage perch.
Before my wheel
a blackbird goes
flying low and shriek
shriek shrieking.

Over The Top Fingertip Tactile

Touching the pitted and lentil-nobbled
    surface of walls;
touching the flat coldness of window glass,
    the muscle smoothness of wood,
the ribbed structure of cloth,
    trouser or chair:
feeling heat and hair coming through skin;
feeling inside curtain folds,
    along linoleum's sharp edges,
between and behind
    knuckle-catching radiators;
locked in touching
    own face,
    own ears,
    own mouth,
    own eyes.

A Counsellor

She asked him
his opinion
only in order
that she
could tell him hers

He spoke.

She began nodding,
waiting
her turn to speak.

Negatives

Grief turned the young man psychotic.
(His brother had recently died.)
He was given maximum sedation
yet all Christmas morning he talked
to God and his brother and he tried
to bang his forehead on the iron bedrail
to knock the images of God and
his dead brother out of his head.
He had moments of pause, of lucidity,
then back to the waking dream.
To stop him damaging himself
I held him to me. He meant me no harm.
And when he cried out to God and
to his brother I quietly told him
where he was and that I was not
God talking to him and that I was not
his brother. I told him that his brother
was dead, again that I was not God;
and from out of his anguish
he smiled kindly on me and said that
he knew that.

Common Denominators

Those who cannot trust
their senses
depend on others
to order their
existence.

But here
in this place of last resort
every ward is the epitome
of existentialism:
patients and staff
change continuously,
so too priorities
and personalities.
Here philosophies
become real questions.
Do I exist?
You?

All fall back
on routines.

Acting Out

Delivered to the asylum at six years of age
we see from his notes that his limited intelligence
was unable to cope with a knowledge of sodomy
beyond his years (then quaintly called
'precocity'.) 54 years on he's still
acting out, walking in circles and
fingerpicking brittle paint off corridor walls.

Abused and confused children continue
to get dumped into the system, only now via
specialised children's units, where
they come up against people who care
what happens to them. The first people
in their pained lives to care about them.
The children soon come to realise
that these people only care because
they were acting mad. So, to be cared for,
and these people have to care
because they are paid to care,
the children go on acting mad. Given time
they'll forget they're acting.

Working With Disturbed Behaviours

The knife is coming my way.
Blunt tableknife
     - handle and blade cast of one metal -
kitchen peeling knife, breadknife, carving knife
     - blackhandled craft knife
     - white polythene sheath with red handle.

The knife is coming my way.
     Knuckleduster smashed jug handle,
     broken lightbulb,
     open scissors
will slice through my cheek,
     gash my chest,
     carve apart my palm,
     cut across my eye,
slit open this belly,
     stab with a thump into my back.

     In all its pained innocence
     the knife is coming my way.

Bleeding

Bleeding has long been considered curative
in that it purges,
purifies.
Menstruation, for instance,
a monthly cleansing of the womb.
And the Masai bleed their cattle.
(That though is for a milk and blood recipe,
 not for the benefit of the animal.)
This other opening of veins
has been to make the bled feel better.
So leeches were attached to arms and legs,
removed with salt when engorged.
Apoplexy, the ague, all could be relieved
by judicious bloodletting.
(Philosophers, politicians and warriors,
 always on the lookout for analogies,
 applied the same remedy to sick nations.
 Without good effect.)
Abused children
(with no knowledge of history
 how do they know to do it?)
still cut themselves
to staunch pain with pain,
make visible the hurt,
simplify the confusion,
to warmly bleed.

Going Under

On a calm morning the sky has
      nicotine coloured clouds.
I drive to work numb and oppressed.

(*Plus ça change la plus ça change.*
The more things change
      the more things change.)

On a wet morning the sunrise is an orange slit
      along a purple and grey horizon.
      As I drive to work I want to cry,
imagine myself in melodramatic tears,
and I go on holding it all back,
breathing hard and holding it all back.

26th February 1988

With a view down the ward corridor,
waiting to go home, for handover to be done,
I stood in the doorway to the long television room.
Patients sat in low chairs down either side.
Some were smoking.
At the far end was the television.
The news was on.

A long distance camera shot
showed three or four Israeli soldiers
on a green hill with two Palestinian boys.
The soldiers picked up rocks and, dropping them,
tried to break the boys' arms.
The soldiers took turns.
I felt sick to the pit of my being.

No patient though, nor waiting nurse,
displayed any undue disgust.
Inured to such atrocities?
Forty minutes it took the soldiers,
        the newsreader said,
to break the boys' arms with the rocks.
This then was not an act of passion,
this was the dogged pursuance of policy.

I looked through the smoke-smeared ward windows
to the tall bleak trees in the asylum grounds,
        and back to the set.
The cameraman had forty minutes of footage.
At gunpoint the boys still
submissively held out their arms
and the soldiers still took turns
        to drop the rocks.

Days Upon Days

With crises and emergencies I can cope:
emptiness it is
that undoes me.

Small worries stretch like glass
distorting
all I see.

Others become irritated by
my unnecessary anxieties.
I worry
about upsetting them.

Squinting through
the attenuated glass,
drymouthed
I wade through years,
hour upon hour,
waiting for mealtimes
which are over
within minutes.

A Mental Nurse

The roundness of her belly gives the game away:
on tubular legs she goes stumping towards her appetite,
tells her charges how good she is to them
and holds them in contempt.

Like all habitual liars
she presumes untruth in all others;
and like all bullies she makes pets
of those who accept her patronage.

Every small incident becomes a drama
with herself as star.
In the throatcatch sentimentality of any of her stories
hers is, unblushingly, always the principal part.

Intruding into every conversation with foghorn insensitivity,
sneaking the patients' food and shouting at them,
you impotently watch - who's going to break rank - her stupidity,
her superstitions and her prejudices shape vulnerable lives.

And you wonder why she works here.
Until you see her beyond the ward, beyond the hospital,
and you see her shrunken
into smallmouthed and frightened insignificance.

Forced into her company though,
watching patients bend before her bombast,
that is a knowledge
difficult to hold on to.

Smalltalk (2)

Was that I heard only that
and not a subliminal instruction?

You've been to a formal gathering,
wanted to make a good impression,
have tried listening to two conversations
at once.

You know how difficult it is,
how one thwarts the other.

Imagine then all those voices
inside a single mind and then you too
ask a question.

Hence the fierce features,
the concentration required to shut out
those other voices
while delivering
a considered
reply.

Alzheimer's Alzheimer's

In a state of waking but never coming awake
     of being left alive with the worry
     of a memory of worry
     of knowing worry
     but not the memory of the worry

I demand a cure for senile dementia
so that people who've had full lives
- lovers, children, careers, histories,
  stories to tell -
can approach death
at least knowing who they are
     who they were

(Alzheimer's going into history
     remembered for a disease
     that makes its victims forget)

£3.89 an hour

Some days I feel like I'll never get clean.
     Not so much the faeces,
     though the smell leaves
     an oyster aftertaste sitting
     in the back of the throat;
     and the shit itself sticks
     to every surface, including skin.
     Nor so much the urine,
     though that seeps and stinks;
     and I can never be sure I haven't
     sat in a chair so tainted.
     No,
     it's the putrefaction,
     death's bad breath,
     the open ulcered wound
     exhaling into my face;
     the rotting flesh on a living body,
     both image and smell that clings.
     Nor can I escape my fear
     of close quarters contagion,
     horror of my becoming
     just such another vacancy.
Some days I feel like I'll never get clean.

No-one's Fault

I know it's conveyor belt treatment not patient-centred care, but it's already 7:30, breakfast's at 8, we're shortstaffed, I've been sent here from another ward, and we've got a 13 hour shift to get through.

The ward sister is getting the female dormitory up singlehanded. The male dormitory is partitioned into 3 bed cubicles, 12 beds altogether. The partitions are of thin board to chest height, one bare narrow shelf per bed. The ward nurse has soft fuzzy hair. She tells me who to get dressed next. I've already got three over to the sink and their teeth cleaned, and the one who's safe is shaving himself.

"Henry'll need a hand. William'll be wet. Bob can manage once he's up."

Their names are taped to the sides of their lockers. Their overwashed clothes are in bundles inside. Today's bundles were made up yesterday. Henry is one of those compact little men, lies there looking up at me with a small smile, eyes puzzled thinking he should know me from somewhere and be pleased to see me.

"I'm going to get you up now Henry." I tell him. Proper professional approach this, telling him each step of getting up what's about to happen to him. I pull the sheets back, swing his legs over the side of the bed and up he comes into sitting position. Henry smiles at me. He isn't wet. I ask him to undo his pyjama top, lift his hands to his buttons, move on to William.

William is a fussy anxious old man, immediately goes stooping to fiddle clawhanded with a knot of bedclothes. Gives me chance to strip off his wet sheets, wipe the mattress with a pillowcase, get his bottoms down before I sit him back on the bed. (Last time I was on this ward I found William worriedly going through the drawers in the nurses' office. He knows he's lost something important. Can't tell him it's his memory.)

Bob is dry. He's a humphy old man. Humphy over nothing in particular, just Humphs. I lay out his clothes beside him, get him started. Henry's hands have dropped from his buttons. He's still smiling at me. I get him undressed. His bundle has net pants, no pad.

"Does Henry have a pad?" I hold up the nets.

"No pad. Must've run out of underpants." She's making beds. I use the net. Bob humphs behind me.

Henry is dressed. I stand him up, look over to the sink,
"Let's get you shaved."

I reach out a hand to his shoulder, see the fist the moment it makes contact. Straight left jab. Bang! My head rocks. Reflex conditioning has me move in close, push him off with my right, bring up my left. Henry is sat smiling on the bed looking bewildered. Already he doesn't remember punching me. Already he doesn't remember me pushing him. My shock and anger though have to out.

"Do that to me again you fuckin little bastard and I'll rip your fuckin head off!"

The nurse with the soft fuzzy hair comes to lead Henry away. He smiles at her, eyes puzzled. "They said he used to box." she says to me; and her tone says, Fancy nice little Henry doing a thing like that. I shake my head. William is plucking apart his new pad.

"I'm going to get you dressed now William." I take the pad from his hands, behind my eyes feel the beginnings of a 12 hour headache.

Pensioner - Female

Bright rain from a white sky greens the day

Old lady, sodden, sits on a plastic chair

In the rot of herself
half-life memories in their decay
she seeks to clothe thoughts
she thinks are there

Love was somewhere. Once

Still it rains

Pensioner - Male

plump pink youth
blinking
shining with student eagerness
praises
the accomplishment of this
bent-legged old man
in caring for himself
at seventy

Asylum Humour (1)

During a civic visit to the local asylum a councillor became separated from his group. Worried by the noise he hurried after them, went through an unmarked door and found himself in the quiet of the asylum grounds. Nearby a man was hoeing some rose-beds. The councillor explained what had happened and asked where he should go. The gardener said that when the visiting group realised that he was missing then a search would be instituted. Easier to find him, therefore, if he stayed in the one place. The councillor agreed with this strategy and sat on a bench among the rose-beds. The gardener returned to his hoeing. The two men started to talk of roses, progressed by stages to world affairs, found themselves in agreement on a variety of topics. Discovering, by a chance remark, that the gardener was a patient and not, as he had assumed, a hospital employee, the councillor asked what he had done that he should have been put into an asylum. The gardener shrugged, said that he had been in the asylum for so many years he doubted that anyone could now remember the original reason for his incarceration.

"This isn't right." The councillor became indignant. "An intelligent man like you should have a home and a garden of your own." The gardener agreed. Whereupon the councillor promised to do all in his power to help the gardener. At that moment the civic group appeared, saw the councillor and beckoned him. The councillor made a note of the gardener's name, said his goodbyes and began walking towards the group, who seemed to be shouting warnings at him. A blow to the back of his head buckled his knees. From the ground he looked up to the gardener, still holding the hoe.

"You won't forget?" he said.

Asylum Equals Sanctuary

Mrs Thatcher said there's no such thing.

Here the hospital managers still do her bidding,
are finishing what she started,
destroying what is already a community
      on the promise of what isn't.

"There is no such thing as society
      only individuals."

Next door to you?
Or here, among friends?

The old Soviet Union used psychiatric hospitals as prisons.
The United Kingdom uses prisons as psychiatric hospitals
      and calls it Community Care.

8,000 A Year In The UK Alone

Crippled by emotion he killed himself at 43.
"Think," friends, exasperated, said to him.
"Think," family, exasperated, said to him.
He couldn't. His thoughts were blocked
      by feelings far too strong.

His mother and father, in their seventies,
      want an explanation.
His wife stares back through the years, stunned.
His children, teenagers, don't understand,
have problems enough of their own
      without his doing this to them;
and, agonised, they look for seeds of suicide
      within themselves.

Asylum Humour (2)

The tyre blew in a rainstorm. The driver didn't have a coat, was drenched by the time he got the jack out of the boot. The road was running with water. Removing the hubcap he wiped some water from his eyes, saw a man sat on a low wall watching him. The man was wearing a woollen dressing gown. The realisation that he had broken down outside the local asylum made the driver nervous. Fumbling he put the wheelnuts in the hubcap, took the wheel to the boot and returned with the spare. Only to find that the hubcap had floated off down the road. He immediately ran after it; but it and the wheelnuts had been washed into a large drain. The driver screamed, shouted, and came stamping and cursing back up the road.

"This car is still capable of being driven," the man in the saturated dressing gown said.

"With three wheels? Get real."

"If you take one nut from each of the remaining wheels," the man calmly continued, "that will give you the same amount of nuts to secure the fourth wheel."

"Brilliant!" the driver shouted. "Absolutely brilliant."

"Mad I may be," the man got off the wall, "Stupid I'm not."

Treatment

So keen on shocking was he
        they called him Jules.
Even his car number was
        6 X ECT.

Case History

His arms hang by his sides and his spine is curved.
Walking from his chair in The Quiet Room,
queuing at the hatch in The Dining Room,
he looks only at the floor before his feet.

He carries the warm plate to his table,
moves the meat and two veg into himself,
takes his stained plate to the dishes trolley
and goes to the hatch to collect his afters.

He empties the bowl into himself,
takes the bowl to the dishes trolley, stacks it,
sits back at the table and waits
to be called to the drugs trolley.

30 years he has been in hospitals,
was first admitted age 22 when,
under pressure of work and a new marriage,
he suffered a 'psychotic episode'.

Earlier in his hospital career he was often pronounced
'better' and returned home. Every time he relapsed.
Each readmission lasted longer. And here he's stayed,
save for occasional experiments in sheltered accommodation.

Out there his wife divorced him.
(No-one blamed her.)
Out there his parents, one soon after the other, died.
In here he seemed not to care.

He missed a lobotomy by a fashion's whisker;
though most other treatments have been tried on him,
even hydrotherapy, so too deep insulin narcosis. He's also
been saturated with vitamins and loaded with dopamine.

According to his drawerful of notes he's had
82 sessions of ECT, the first 6 without anaesthetic.
Chlorpromazine continues to be the favoured drug;
although when loud and high he's known paraldehyde.

For a time, back there, he became addicted
to a prescribed benzodiazepine. To no good effect.
For the last 2 years he's been on a fortnightly depot
and, to counter its side effects, a daily Procyclidine.

Now his time is filled with art therapy,
                occupational therapy
                and helping in the garden.

But where the man?
Where the man of 30 years before?
Where the man who had a job and a woman wanting to marry him?
Where the man before he came to this place, these treatments?

White tablet swallowed, taking small steps,
avoiding all physical contact, eye contact,
arms hanging by his side, spine curved,
he goes to his chair in The Quiet Room.

Dinosaurs

On the back wards in grey suits
was where the dinosaurs lurked,
leftovers from pre-psychotropic times,
an age of padded cells and straitjackets,
when a nurse without sedatives
had to prove fitness for the job
by fighting inmates.
   Behaviourism at its most basic:
   hit me and get hit.
Except that the psychopaths didn't learn,
others forgot
and so every working day had been down
to hit-or-be-hit survival.
Hard for them later to empathise
with those still seen as threats.
Dinosaurs thus had no truck
   with psychotherapy
   and the cult of self.

Instant Ghost

Smiling at a remark
I pick up the phone.

"Had to force entry."
the policeman says.

"Found your man
 hanging from the stairs.

He's quite cold."

There But For The...

Excessive dopamine in the brain impedes the neurotransmitters,
which can result in the afflicted believing that, just by
being looked at, others can affect their thoughts; and that
inside their skulls are antennae for the individual reception
of TV and radio signals.

> Is this it?
> Is this it?
> When a waffling spokesman
> comes on the radio
> I know, I know
> what is going to be said next.

> Is this it?
> Is this it?
> When my grey cat wants to be fed
> he sits nearby
> and sends me messages
> via his golden eyes.

In This World

In this world of shared illusions, to those excluded
because their senses cannot make sense of the everyday,

the very illogicality of religion appeals. Intuition
can be truth; invisible deities and miracles nothing

out of the ordinary. (Cults thrive on the fringes
of sense. Some actually target such susceptibility.)

This, however, has an innocence. Because, come
Sunday morning, bodies go from dormitory to dormitory,

ward to ward, rousing late-sleepers and making
their own procession through the corridors

some of the women hatted and begloved, some men
for once straight-backed, some even brylcreemed.

(This is how it is, is what I've seen; is not
my intention to patronize. Immunity there is none,

as well smile pityingly on myself.) At the chapel door
fags are properly topped and stubbed.

Depressive Illogic

Sentimental illusions unfostered have I.
Immune deficiencies unacquired have I.
Open an artery?
Cleanse the flesh?
Unspark the neural synapse?
Cheat the virus of its victim?
Win?

Whence that arrogance that knew that I alone was right?
Whence that bravery that welcomed any fight?
Did I ever exist?

Meanings

Tracker ancestors,
stooped men in leather leggings,
have left us the legacy
of looking for meanings in things;
in words, in gifts, in unconnected events.
So we look for significance
in expressionless stares,
in faces that are turned away,
in smiles that are switched off,
caresses witheld, commonplaces unspoken.
A whole day can be haunted
by a single word clumsily said,
or used intentionally to hurt,
and succeeding.
That one word cleaved into the mind
like the image of a livid wound.

In the Geography of the Head

To enter the arena of another's madness
you first have to be certain who you are.

She is fat and she says
clouds are mirrors and the moon is a hole
that lets light through from the sun.
Gravity is hell, she says,
and draws diagrams in red biro
of round eyeballs and sharp points of focus.

I'm not about to argue
or to agree with her.

Singleminded

"I am the world."
            the patient says.
"What is happening to me?"

a coprophilous nurse
concentrates on the bowels
            - ease of evacuation,
size and consistency of stools

"I am the world."
            the patient says.
"What is happening to me?"

Micturition Syncope *(fainting while pissing)*

Awareness crawls in biostatic over the unseen grey
      of a walnut-wrinkled cerebrum:
a self-regarding series
of electro-chemical reactions that add up
      self-consciously
      to The Self.
Dreams are collections and creations
of those roaming sparks,
generate their own random order,
sense making sense of sense.
      I once was seed now am man,
      seed of seed of seeds,
dictators of my shapes and diseases.

Seeds though are not continuums.
Succession comes in understandings
      passed on.
Strangers will be my heirs.

This seed, sower of seeds, reaper of understandings,
this unique collection of synapses,
wakes
in dawn's literal light
on the bathroom floor
      head halfway out the bathroom door.

Wide-eyed and wondering
      I look up at pipes and paintings
      in shades of grey. I realise
after a few moments
      that I have no memory of fainting.
And I know now, with relief,
how it is to die.
      It is not to know.

As The Asylum Closes

As the asylum closes
- ward by ward being shut down, the few
  continuing in use clustered about
  the doctors' offices, canteen and shop -
the building itself
is coming to mimic the condition
of its once inmates - imposing facade,
but empty inside, barely functional.

To walk the still shined corridors
is to experience, as with the patients,
a sense of profound waste: these long indoor tunnels
oddly uninhabited;
with - behind unlabelled doors -
wards noiseless and vacant.

Patients are flesh and blood ghosts of what might have been:
this building a misplaced opportunity, ghost of a chance.

No caterwauling spectres will haunt these corridors:
every stone will be removed,
the passing of a hundred years of feet, of as many hands
trailed along walls, erased.
Here, among these crisp green fields, will be built instead
another neat redbrick estate with, for all the emotions
that have ranged here, street names anodyne.

Within this building was company and safety.
Beyond here,
isolated,
loneliness will press black against all windows.

Crowds

Mouths open, grins agape, looking over the shoulders of those
in front, mouths open, grins agape, looking over the shoulders
of those in front, mouths open, grins agape, looking over the
shoulders of those in front at a desperate soul making a fool
of himself. (Not for their amusement: he needs them only to
complete the circle of his abasement.) Mouths open, grins
agape, looking over the shoulders of those in front, mouths
open, grins agape, looking over the shoulders of those in front,
they watch the man digging out his one psychotic word.
"Yes
Yes
Yes
Yes

Survivors

Having survived suicide,
having already killed the Self,
what does the victim then build upon?
With whom?
Those ghosts of wife or husband
who were of the unlivable past?
Life, looking forward life,
ended with that first attempt.
Subsequent repeated suicide bids
are just a matter of getting rid
of the troublesome stubborn body;
and each new try is bungled because,
in this after-life,
in these days of impinging dreams,
there's no real conviction, no urgency.

Emotional Stunting

I cannot understand you because I don't know
if what you say is true.
Life lies to me. Rocks and buses
take on significances which don't make sense.

With senses not to be trusted I stick to routines,
to conversations that are catechisms. I can take no
interest in another's life, have to make sure only
that I say and do what is expected of me.

Mine is a narrow path. Any step to the side
is into the uncharted, the unsafe. I cannot trust
what the un-authorised say. I cannot trust what
the authorised remark upon beyond their brief.

They must utter the prescribed response, fulfill
only my expectations of them. Should they
be talking of other matters I will wait. I may
seem self-centred, selfish, my world though
                    is myself.

When all perceptions are jangled, when what I see, hear,
can be images, sounds, ideas internally manufactured,
understand me, my perspective entire is altered.
Understand me: I am incapable of understanding you.

Exercise Bike

Something happened
to make me thin:
not a fashion magazine
I'm distorted
trapped within.

(Anorexic
      with a sly greed
      for emptiness
      in ward corners
      crams laxatives,
      swallows ripped Kleenex;
      sneaks to squeaking
      exercise bike,
      wincing burns off
      the imposed and suffusing
      contractual calories.)

Mummy Daddy
love me
love each other
and I will be well.

Full Circle

The Frenchman, Philipe Pinel, in the 1790s removed the mentally ill from the freak shows and their chains. (An observer noted how, though unshackled, the subjects remained attached to their chains. So do zoo animals, a later behaviourist attested, continue to pace before the opened door of their cages.)

The new asylums of the 1890s were enclosed within cages. These both barred voyeuristic visitors and protected the public from the excesses of the insane. Although sexually segregated within the building, the asylum offered a freedom of sorts - to be mad. Many asylums were self-sufficient, had farms, gardens, laundries run by the inmates; and, for management of their extreme selves, straitjackets and padded cells.

With the advent, in the 1950s, of neuroleptic drugs, the bars were removed, the wards unlocked, cells unpadded, and the asylums were renamed mental hospitals. Newly disturbed people were admitted for diagnosis and treatment. (Note - treatment and not cure. Mental illness is a condition not a disease. Hospital is therefore a misnomer; and semantics is all in psychiatry.) With the condition now locked within themselves, unnoticed, unmarked, the afflicted had no need of residency, could make do with outpatient, respite, relapse visits.

Now, in he 1990s, with the asylums being closed, anonymous town houses have replaced asylum wards. These small houses are underfunded, understaffed, under-inspected. Difficult patients are easiest managed - by the undertrained staff - by the locking of doors. The most troublesome are unseen tied to their beds. (The universality of television, of horror videos, means that the public no longer need to visit freak shows.) Full circle.

Define Personality

We are our brains
Should a car accident
    or mugging
damage the hypothalamus
the injured thereafter
will be full of
    a limping rage
will spend the remainder
of their shuffling days
chemically contained

Built-in Obsolescence

Cancers within us all
wait to be called

    Voices used are
        alcohol
        nicotine
        pollution
        stress

Detonations in minds
await triggers

    Provocations are
        divorce
        grief
        loss of job or virginity
        loneliness

Raised

generations
raised to believe
the body's desires
profane...

all itches
though must be
scratched
or they bury
themselves deep
in the psyche
where fingernails
can't reach

to enter
madness can be
the only escape
from abuses suffered
within this society's
sacred family

but to belong
here is not to belong
- by categorising ourselves
mad, beyond here
we make of ourselves
outcasts

Humanism Is On The Ebb

"The history of psychiatry is essentially the history of humanism. Every time humanism has diminished or degenerated into mere philanthropic sentimentality, psychiatry has entered a new ebb. Every time the spirit of humanism has arisen, a new contribution to psychiatry has been made."
Gregory Zilboorge.

Humanism is on the ebb.
The asylums are closing and the police cells are full.
Humanism is on the ebb.
A condition is again a crime, treatment's unavailable.
Humanism is on the ebb.
The institutionalised have gone
from walking the asylum corridors
to walking the corridors of the streets.
Round and about,
up and down,
there and back.
Round and about,
up and down,
there and back
inhabiting realms and prisons inside themselves,
inside themselves.
Both feared
and victims of fear:
there are no secular havens,
nowhere else to go.
Humanism is on the ebb.
Humanism is on the ebb.

The New Asylum

purpose-built bungaloid brick
bodged by budgets
          all is clean paint
          keys and carpets
Soundproofed doors mean
screams cannot be heard
alarm sirens seem
designed to confuse
private rooms mean
assaults cannot be seen
          communal rooms
          so small
          one other
          makes a crowd
do not, easily overheard, invite
the crucial confidence
          pained disclosure
          that might tell some
          if not all
          hearing nothing
here is treated only
the chemistry of thought
not its social situation
          Public perception
          and stigma
          stay the same
What's changed?
          Understaffed
no grounds, doors locked
we new attendants wait
          listen hard

Before Neuroleptics

Before neuroleptics
was containment and cleanliness
the rigid ordering of time:
men went to the right of the asylum
women to the left.
In the exercise yard
circling
counting bars
she knew she'd win.
(An old woman now
 in the comfort of the new asylum
 she is telling this story
 to some new inmates)
Circling in that yard
a plane had gone overhead
and hers had been the only face
that had looked up.
She had known then
that she'd win.
(Heartstring sentimentality
 of the story form
 creates bogus endings.
 Not one of the new inmates
 sat around the television
 thought to ask
 if she was here
 what she'd won)

In The Carpeted Corridor...

blotched naked
a step from her door
the whole of her sagging
jowls downwards
"I'm lost." she says
looking beseeching up
from the bend in her neck
like old women do.

Taking the tissue-soft arm
I turn her around
"Here you are.
 This one's your room."
"No." she pulls feebly from me
"You don't understand."
The old eyes can't hold mine
"You don't understand.
  It's myself I've lost."

It's A Wage

Working days are haunted by the smell of something stepped on. Psychiatry now is a garage put among a web of pitted roads and blind junctions. Any cars, that happen to make it to the garage, get mended; are sent out to become damaged again. Mechanics, who thought more of their cars than their income, would campaign for better roads. Madness, though, can never be self-diagnosed. These mind-physicians won't heal themselves.

Problems & Polemics

PrOblEMS and POlEMicS

in

controVERSial discoursE

with

VicARIOUS efFects and nORMS

SymptOMs And PSYCHosEs

COntra-indicationS of medicaTion

aLternatIVE/remeDIEs

PRaise and prOmiSEs

MANipulation by puNishmEnt and Reward

QUESTion FAcULTY and function

FORGet One's own

HUMan fallibILITY

Two Men On A Cricket Field

Rain stopped,
let off the ward for a walk,
medication taking effect he is also
unsteady after a week's inactivity.
A pretence of concern has me
keep him within arm's reach.

We make it across the carpark,
without him accosting any visitors,
and down the steps between the laurels
to the cricket pitch.

Away across the far side
is a rusting roller, sight screens
parked below an oak.
At grass height
swallows are skimming
the glistening wicket,
seeming to tip between daisy heads.
Flickers of consciousness - that know
the way to Africa and back -
they flick between and about
us two ambling mammals.

Events, things, in a psychotic state,
are supercharged with significance.

Especially the self-generated. He stubs a finger on his forehead,
"The I that inhabits this world
  inside my own head..."
he glares into my eyes (ward behaviour),
"...is not the I
  who sometimes comes into the world
  inside your head."
Stepping around his apparent aggression
I turn him with me.
"Why don't these swallows crash
  into the grass?" I ask.
"The swallows?"
he steps after me, says,
"Yes. The swallows."

Where The Sense In This?

In 1982
on a warship off the Falklands
six men sat in the Petty Officers Mess.
A seventh man, leaning in the doorway,
was talking with the others when
an Exocet missile came through the wall
and removed his head on its way
to the torpedo room.
Six Petty Officers survived the explosion
to tell this story over and over again.

Most Often

First and foremost, for most of us,
the mentally ill are unpredictable
- in so far as we have come to expect
  reactions from a whole range of people
  who are said not to be mentally ill.
The different are always considered dangerous;
danger equals excitement; thus the different
come to attract and repel in equal measure.
Those writers of fiction, who are unconsciously
confident of their sanity, exploit this
inner otherness. Not, though, to depict
mental illness. No, their use becomes
a celebration, a glamourisation of insanity
- exotic as a tropic to a temperate people
  (yet, as we all know, in humdrum hot places
  ordinary people try to live ordinary lives).
These writers only use madness to free themselves
from the constraints of the normal, madness
allowing them to ditch imprisoning expectations
of plot and stereotyped character (such use
becoming a display, note, not of imagination,
but of its lack). On their pages the demented
and the deranged can safely threaten an everyday
accepted view of life - everything in its place
and all's well with an unequal world. Yet,
most often, the mentally ill will seek
unqualified acceptance within the very status quo
that the campaigning writer of fictions
wants changed.

Case Study (1)

He made animal noises. Started
when he had a job, sweeper up,
in a paper mill. On breaks,
away from the clatter, rattle and hiss,
out in the sun men leant back
against the warm tin
of the green corrugated walls
and smoked their cigarettes. One
of the men
remembered, from primary school, that
the sweeper then used to make animal noises
          - a moo, a snuffling grunt, a neigh.
The sweeper saw the men laughing at
the faces he pulled, at the sounds he made,
made more.
          Sweeping up the wet alleyways
between the big iron machines, he stopped
close behind men, and made animal noises.
Some men smiled, some shrugged busily
away. One, startled, turned and,
in temper, hit. Got hit back
with the broom. Both men
were sacked. At home
he made mournful animal noises.
His mother called the doctor. In hospital
he was injected. Was quiet.
Back home he began to go out
the day his injection
was due. His mother shouted
at him. To tease her
he made animal noises. She
called the doctor. In hospital
he was injected. Was quiet.

Heat

Skin,
all types and colour,
largest organ
of the human body,
goes, with a cooking glaze,
shiny on the burn,
is an instant livid brand.
A scald, however,
attracts to it
lymphatic fluid
to wobble under blisters.
(So too certain fever spots
 and the chemical stings
 of dung fly and jellyfish.)

On an asylum back ward
a patient filled his own bath
and jumped in.
      His unnatural screams
brought the male nurse running.
The bathwater was almost boiling.
      The nurse
went to pull out the patient,
but the boiled skin
came away in his hands.
      He jerked out
the bathplug's hot chain;
but the sloughed layers
of white tissue
stopped the drain-hole.
      By which time

shock had killed the patient.
(The nurse still sweats
 in the telling of this tale;
the remembered excitement
- to trigger the exocrine glands -
having increased his body temperature
to in excess of 34.5 centigrade.)

Incident 1

The nursing assistant is sat on a low chair in the office, door open, reading through the new patient's old notes. A staff nurse is sat up at the desk, plastic nursing files beside her, writing up the shift. The new patient - a shuffling man in his late fifties, grey suit over-washed - was dropped on the ward along with his lifetime stack of notes. Shown his bed, his property checked, he went straight in to lunch. "Says here," the nursing assistant waits until the staff nurse indicates that she is listening, "this new guy throws hot food over other people." From the dining room comes a man's shout of surprise and a woman's scream.

One Time Called Hysteria

nameless she's a vacancy
her father's daughter, husband's wife
her children's mother, house's keeper
her clothes, her shape

Keeps her busy

children grown leave home
clothes don't fit
her changed shape
husband can't wait
to leave this non-woman

her parents die. She can't
afford new clothes, becomes
aware at last
of the absence of a self

in her outside life
she develops an illness
and becomes it

The Loneliness of Pain

Depression can manifest itself as
hypochondria: the person wanting to be ill,
illness explaining what is fundamentally
at fault with their world.
In proving that they are unwell, however,
their own dignity gets overlooked.
(Dignity being what they must look like
  to others; their being so peevish, so
  petulant, carping, complaining,
  seeking to shift blame off themselves
  for the failure of every suggested future.)
Blunted by anxiety, all is truncated,
walks and thoughts dragging them back
to a non-centre.
Resisting all help, so can the shakes
and aches of pharmacologically-induced
parkinsonia get dismissed as symptomatic
of their complaining nature. Likewise
side-effect tardive dyskenesia or
ocular gyrocrisis. This ignoring
of their very real discomfort
reinforces their belief that there
really is something terribly wrong
that they are not being told.

Case Study (2)

If, when he attacked his neighbour,
he had been tried for assault,
had paid his fine, done his time;
if his brother had told someone, then,
that the old woman next door
did persecute him, did
bang on the dividing wall, did lay
in wait and berate him, did pull faces,
make vile gestures at him every single time
she saw him passing her window; if his brother
had said that he too had seen this,
instead of saying that his brother had always
'taken things too much to heart';
then he wouldn't have been diagnosed initially
as suffering paranoid delusions
and placed on a Section. If
we had believed him when he quietly told us
how much the hospital beds were hurting his back
and if the doctors hadn't thought his anger
at being disbelieved a part of his delusion;

if we had paid more attention to his complaints
about the effects the neuroleptics were having on him
he wouldn't have tried to squeeze himself
through the first-floor window; and if,
before he came back from the secure unit,
they had told us that two days previously
he had tried to strangle a woman he thought
'was about to attack me'; and if his brother
had said that he had phoned him every week
since his admission threatening suicide;
if we had understood what he meant when he said
that the fortnightly depots
were leaving him 'no future', that they wouldn't
let him 'have two thoughts together',
then maybe he wouldn't have been allowed
to proceed on weekend leave, to the same flat
beside the horrible old woman; and maybe
he wouldn't, within three hours of getting indoors,
have hung himself. Maybe.

Incipients All

Madness is everyone's experience:
from a single word clue
thinking "You too." You too
have known this - this state of mind:
psychotic lapses like vivid dreams,
drunken adventures that stay forever
just beyond complete recall.
        Or is this playing mad?
The imagination made singular? Imitating
in public the parts most only dare play
in front of mirrors? And, out of
new habit, acting on the single-minded
impulses of a toper; forgetting one,
pursuing another..?
        Here
some nurses and doctors,
intimates of death and nakedness,
become engrossed in the dissection
of thought, analysis of the thinking
process (or they become filing clerks
looking for labels), who nonetheless
assume themselves to be
superior to their patients, because
they have not lately looked below
the surface of human actions
and watched their own
selves behave. They too
repeat their mistakes. Incipients all.

We

In the bleak uncertainty of reason,
beyond courtesy, and manners, in the

not-quite-connectedness of this universe,
it is our madnesses that we share.

> They dissect cats
> to find out
> what makes people sick.

A conceit of the self-declared sane
is that they control their own existence:

they were taught to ask the right questions
- the ones the teachers can answer.

> They study rats
> to find out what
> makes people tick.
> (Then seek ways to
> turn people into rats.)

While here we are
- shouting in the streets or,
incomprehensible to ourselves
in the comfort of asylums
- the last pagans.

We All Swim In The One Sea

Psychiatry cannot be isolated
from the society it serves:
mental illness is a disease
primarily of the powerless,
even suicides seen as symptomatic
of sociological states, despair
as a statistic. Because someone
may be in hospital doesn't mean
that they are ill: often they are
assumed to be unwell solely because
they are in hospital. So do doctors
and nurses become accomplices to
insanity, reliant for a living
upon their own diagnoses.

Into Themselves

Into themselves
children take their family's conflicts,
become ill,
starve or cut themselves,
become as disorderly as the family.
    Follow the broken glass.

Into themselves
adults take society's imbalance,
become ill
or outcasts, criminals or drunks,
add to society's dislocation.
    Follow the broken glass.

Into themselves
survivors take war's hatreds,
become ill,
hate themselves for having killed,
or for having been afraid to fight back,
carry their hatreds into the next war.
    Follow the broken glass.

Case Study (3)

They looked what they were - an old farming couple. From her bun to her forearms she was big and round. He, flat-capped, was bent over with arthritis. Their son was already running the farm. So it was the sensible thing to do: he needed to be given a free hand, his wife needed to have the kitchen to herself. The green-mossed house was big enough to have had part converted into a flat; but she said the young ones didn't need them watching all their doings. And she needed to get away, she said, from the stink of diesel and dung; didn't want to be woken six every morning by the tractor starting up, the wet shuffle of cows on concrete, the clanging of gates and parlour stalls, the drone of the milk pump. "Gets into my head," she said.

So they moved down to the town, bought a bungalow in a cul-de-sac. "Be nice to have neighbours near by," she said. But these weren't farming neighbours, dropping by to borrow gear, stopping off for a cup of tea and a natter. These town neighbours were nine-to-fivers, had their own lives evenings and weekends. She was left looking out at silence.

And still she was woken at six, or earlier, by her husband groaning up to take his painkillers; and when he didn't she woke anyway. To silence.

After breakfast he went off most days to look at his one field of bullocks, ended up usually back at the farm. As did her other sons and daughters. She went up there for tea on Sundays, with them all, as before. She said she liked what they'd done to the kitchen, complained about the stink of diesel and dung, the damp chill of the old house.

Only when they remembered did her grown children call in at the bungalow. It was so small, they said, they were frightened of knocking things over. Even her youngest daughter didn't stop long. When she went, she waved goodbye from the garden gate, like she had imagined, and she was left in silence.

She knew she had made a mistake and that there was no going back: leaving the farm had been the sensible thing to do.

Farmers are used to killing, a logical solution to many a livestock problem. She decided, therefore, to kill herself; but she didn't want any of her family or her old farming neighbours to find her. So she took a bus to the next town, sat on a bench beside a stream and swallowed all her husband's painkillers.

She was found, taken to hospital, revived and transferred - for her own safety - to the asylum. She had been the force in the family, the one who'd made the decisions. None, visiting, could thus argue with her now, just wept to see her there, shouting angry at having survived.

Sedated, apparently calm, she was allowed to return home, to the bungalow. Within a week she caught a bus to another town, took another overdose. Was found.

And this became the pattern of her admissions; with each admission taking longer, because each admission she was madder at being there, flinging off the nurses who tried to give her sedating injections, cursing them with whatever nonsense came into her head. When these peculiar curses were repeated back to her later, asked what she had meant, she said, "Well I was just talking rubbish," and she chuckled in her fat farmer's wife way. She was given ECT. Which sent her high.

Yet still, although pressed by all and sundry, she wouldn't return to live at the farm. A sensible decision had been made and had to be stuck by. She did go to the farm though for Christmas leave. The relatives all promised the doctors they'd keep an eye on her, watch out for tablets, make sure she didn't leave the house unaccompanied. Nor did she. After lunch Boxing Day she took herself off to the room in the house furthest from anyone else. It was used as a store. She hung herself from a dust-furred beam. She didn't leave a note.

Can Carriers And Coverers Of Backs

Once fingertips dig into wrist,
count the dum de-dum de-dum
of mammal being then
that tremulous life is his
is her responsibility.

Now say after me
"Sorry,
 according to our tick-list
 we no longer have to assist
 you in your efforts to exist."

Politics of medicine now
condemns its victims
to a life beyond death.
Politics of medicine now
already allows
the foetus of a possible Beethoven
or a Christy Brown
to be cancelled.
Killed, that is.

Once living, however,
our own selfish survival greed,
one more moment, one more gulp,
won't let go.
Nor will
our own selfish love
- watching them collapse
 inwardly through the black hole
 of their mouth into death -
let them go.

Gasping cadavers
grey-to-yellow skin sinking
and clinging to flaking bones;
if these lives prolonged beyond pain

beyond thought
were dogs
doctors, nurses would be
prosecuted for cruelty.

Betubed, bewired
pumped full of steroids and air,
bowels irrigated, catheterised,
hands become claws;
if this consciousness of grunts
in the register of pain

of non-pain
was an embryo and not old
it'd be aborted.

Go then.

Let go.

But make the decision your own, now,
don't inflict it on another
later.

Case Study (4)

He is a hopper whose modus operandi has become
a real illness, but of the wrong kind
                    with the wrong result.
        He had it off
to a fine art, had dropped in on hospitals
as far apart as Aberdeen and
                    Penzance.
            Began his career
with a simple deep gash into arm or leg. For which
he was given TLC and stitches, told to come back
                    in a week.
        Such occasional encounters, though,
didn't satisfy his psychological need to be
the centre of kindly nurse attention, the butt
of dark but manly humour from duty doctors.
        So, using novocaine and scalpel
(both bought legally over the counter), he cut
into a ligament at the back of his knee. This
required surgery, a plaster cast and a hospital
stay.
        Worked twice. But, thereafter,
doctors began to recognise the handiwork of doctors
            and to wonder at this body of scars.
        Realising that the game was up
he began to vary his admissions by chopping off
bits of fingers, again with novocaine and scalpel.
        His description and MO were, by now,
being circulated on the Munchausen memo. Made no
difference: jeans drenched in blood he fell through
        the door of yet another A&E.
            Being recognised

the on-call psychiatrist was summoned. Curious
rather than condemning, he had him admitted
to the local asylum. Where a chart was compiled
of his trips and hospital visits, costs to
the Health Service calculated, excluding
Disability Allowance, in excess of
six hundred thousand pounds.
    Although
    Munchausen Syndrome is not
specifically a psychiatric disorder
he was deemed a threat to himself and
    to the safety of others
    and detained under the Mental Health Act.
One might've supposed he'd be pleased;
but these, in the asylum, were the wrong kind
of doctors, made no jokes, only asked why.
    And the nurses here didn't cater
    to his comfort, didn't smile sweetly
on his bravery, pity him his pain, Rather
    they looked
sideways at him, trying to figure out his game. So
seeking transfer to a 'proper' hospital, only way
he knew how, but here without benefit of novocaine,
he bit into one of his three remaining fingers,
had chewed it to the bone before an ambulance
    was called.
    Face smeared in gore, however, and with
the label 'auto-cannibalism' attached, a horrified
A&E sister quickly dressed the stump and he was sent
    straight back.
    To the wrong kind of nursing attention.

Too Much

Too much for a single mind to order,
to keep tabs on, to keep track of, to bear.
     So the single mind lets go,
     slips deliberately
     into degradation.

Daring itself do its worst
it courts incontinence,
     debases itself,
     defaces itself,
     defames itself.

When the single mind believes itself
     sufficiently punished
     for the self-indulgence of letting go
     it feigns amnesia
     and slowly reasserts control,
     piece by laundered piece.

     And yet, and yet
     she sits there
in the stink of her incontinence
while white lights of anger and despair
pop and burst inside her belly and her legs.

     Control?

Male Nurse

As soon as you become a psychiatric nurse
all of your extended family will start having
nervous breakdowns. They will either
get put on beta-blockers, or anti-depressants,
and they will want you to let them know
the side-effects of their medication.
And every other person you now meet will want
to tell you, at length, about their ex
who hung, gassed or, in some novel way,
otherwise killed themself. Or, watching
for your reactions, they will confide how they
themselves were sexually abused, are still
having therapy. Even your new colleagues
will seem to court disaster in their affairs
and marriages. On top of all that, after a year
you will be going to work in second-hand shirts
and be buying your shoes and trousers in
the sales. The puzzle of people, yourself included,
is what will keep you in the job.

**Walking from Seaton to Lyme Regis
the day after Vera died**

Beyond bracken, gorse
and grey sea views,
once in the woods we're
on the undercliff.

We are about half way
and it is always raining.
The path winds
back and forth,
nothing to see but trees
and slippery path.

We're lost though
we know where we are
- cliffs above,
  sea below -
too far along to go back
and not there yet.

Ritual & Belief

To appreciate the satisfaction offered by ritual
watch any man, or woman, line up their tools
prior to starting their work. Expertise, plus effort
and time taken, will result in the belief
of a job well done. Such can also be
demonstrated by those patients who are offered
ECT as a last and drastic measure. The degree
of their desperation, the stronger their belief
in it is, the more susceptible they will be to
the attendant rituals of the pre-treatment fast,
the theatre of the waiting room musak, sight
of the altar-like trolley bed and its ministering
anaesthetist. (Needles, machines, wires and
monitors will complete the sense of ceremony.)
Comes the rush of unconsciousness, the confused
awakening in another room, instant tears or
euphoria. (The more the patient wants to believe
in the treatment the more likely they are
to believe themselves cured and to act
as if cured.)

Case Study (5)

Broad back hunched over spiked mat
of wire-grey hair, eyebrows and cheeks
corrugated with white scar tissue, nose
flattened, the thick loose lips
as much as the short bowed legs
give him the look of a troll. Added to which
big hands hang off his long arms.
Quick to tantrums
he hits. He has fits.
In jovial mood he likes to play
mathematical tricks,
asks for a number, adds three,
multiplies, divides by six;
"Is it below or above..?"
He tells you that
the number you first thought of
is... He has fits.
In his word games, leering and
chuckling, the answer is always
"it". He has fits.
The one surviving relative, his mother,
is too frail to visit. He has fits.
A clonic cry and jerk brings his face
slap flat on the table top. The body,
clenched around the convulsion, rocks,
locked and balanced on the hard seat
of the dining chair. The legs, in spasm,
have the feet drum; and, from the bronchial
grunting of the chest, from the gurgling larynx,
come leaking engine noises. This is how,
untended, he will die. He has fits.

Civilised Structures

Streets of glass carry their intestines
beneath a scratch-frosted camber.
Through black & white roots of lace
like pulse-less capillaries
lie sewage and water pipes
in straight lines. Here,
in a symphony of T-junctions,
can be seen the connectedness of insular lives.
(Fear, still, of cholera
 keeps waste and water distinctly apart.)

Following maps in the head
- of back alleys and micro-circuits
   and always at the edge of the page -
whole lives will be done in units of one.
Male lives built around happy ideas:
here-and-now contact ducked from,
existences being created through the mail,
via radio or the internet.
Fax is OK. Phone too direct.

Their pavements - small journies of necessity,
collection of provisions -
are hard squared places
with unkind thoughts and side-looking faces.
The street's schizophrenic,
surprised in conversation with himself,
will scream at the sky,
frightening them passing by,
always passing by,
insides blistered with fright burns.
Home was a map eighteen pages back.

2 Rape Victims

Bending double the young man holds his arms to his sides and runs at the window. His head through the broken pane he tries to saw his head off. The remaining shards catch in the skin of his neck and they either snap or get dislodged from their old putty groove. Bleeding nonetheless, and having so dramatically begun his suicide he cannot now stop, he runs from the house, into the main road, and he dives in front of a lorry. The massive smoking tyres miss him. He scrambles out from underneath the dirty lorry and into the next lane. A car brakes on his chest, leaves a tyre mark. But he is still breathing. A filter lane further on has not yet come to a stop. He leaps in front of the next car. The bonnet catches his legs. He crashes sideways in through the windscreen. The driver, an old man, stares pop-eyed at him. (Men have got out of their cars and vans and have chased him.) Hands grab hold of his protruding legs. Others reach in to pin him down among the glass chips. All watch the old man grunt and choke into death.

Jigsaws & Crosswords

The young, being new, lay claim to every new idea; albeit that those ideas have usually been a long time coming. These bright-eyed young, however, having just found their place, having just realised their power to change, to alter the very societies that have shaped them, they want to take charge of what's due. The past can only belong to the past: these young don't question what's gone. No, these firm-fleshed young purposefully grasp their every chance. Ambition never satisfied they seek out new challenges, to forcefully take control. Of what? Later they will try to piece together what happened, why it led to where it did. This ordinariness. The only non-doubt they will then have is that they were used. To good intent or by a criminal element they will be unable to decide. Old age always finds for itself puzzles.

On The Edge Of Light
(for Shelley)

One petal blink
of a camera shutter:
this snapshot present
enters a future.

On the edge of light
darkness is infinite
             Maybe

In the ghetto
of my years
I own an old man's
impatience with
pandering fools.

On the edge of light
is the deepest water
             Maybe

Off-camera the wolves
of decrepitude
are circling in.

On the edge of light
is the vertigo of forever
             Maybe

You, Nurse

You, nurse, have learnt not to flinch
from stinks or deformities. The horrors,
you know, belong to unfamiliarity,
to imagination's exaggerations. A rounded
stump of a leg, the stunted hands
of a flame-scarred man; or women
with plastic holes in their abdomens
are all a matter of fact when daily
treating with them. You, nurse,
while at work keep all your emotions
tamped down, show the world only
your public face. (Innermost thoughts
can occasionally be surprised in a blush,
or a blink-backed tear.) You, nurse,
of all the futures that you imagine
for yourself, the one you don't consider
is that fifteen years hence you will
still be in the same place dreaming
the same dreams.

Timing

Answering an advert I got to be one of those
doing the holding down. Though I could,
as easily, have been the one being held down,
my bum crack exposed, needle being slowly
slowly pushed in to the upper-outer buttock
quadrant. If I hadn't stopped drinking, if
I'd taken a pill, a punch, a drag too many...
Locked into a role, any role, temptation is
always to make one's life again more random,
open it again to chance.
So does the death-squad assassin
step beyond his brief, stop the next stranger.

Case Study (6)

the staff nurse comes back/ as patient
to the hospital where once/ she worked
where, as nurse, she felt/ disconnected
from all around her/ she knows now they are
telling each other they knew her/ but didn't
because it is enough for most people
to know each other's names/ say them
at every meeting
and such friendships need, usually,/ go no further
but here, now, these nurses have to proceed
               to an intimacy
               unfounded in friendship
(friendship would breach the professional distance)
sympathy, yes, but that was her undoing
               back then she thinks
here, now, she has to shape that past
               to fit what has followed
she knows she confused herself
could not reconcile sympathy
               for her patients' confused states
               with intolerance for their
                    unsociable behaviours
               for their smelly self-neglect
all of her, she knows, she thinks she knows
was built on faulty experiences
               trained as a child to read
               and repeat but not to think
she knows, thinks she knows
there can be no more pleasantly/ fooling herself
with humorous (maybe) misconceptions
               prudish euphemisms
knowledge, clear and precise,/ has to be hers
but here, now, the only certainty she owns
               is that some life goes on/ must go on

Old People Sit Like Lizards
For Hours Without Moving

Any visitor
is picked
clean of news

Visitor left
they have only
their window reflection
to tell it to

Time is a riddle
through which life dribbles

Cupboards tidied
mementoes are rediscovered
of pasts forgotten
puzzled over

Replaced
are forgotten again

Time is a riddle
through which life dribbles

Case Study (7)

movement is a search her legs make
nothing purposeful   small
compulsive steps   she moves
cannot stop   finish any task
                    even a bath
                    walks around
inside a comet trail
of her own stink   her life
is going to pieces
                    around her
she can't find things she put down
                    a minute ago
let alone herself   if
briefly sat   she moves rather than
let another lean into the column
                    of her rising smell
                    entering a room
she notes the increase in volume   knows
that they were talking about her
before she came in (when she came in
 one, loudly, changed the topic; another,
 loudly, responded) she doesn't like them
either   walks in a circle
                    and leaves
                    she lives now
among people who don't put the lids
back on things   she goes
from room to room putting the lids
back on things
                    forgets
                    moves

No Problem

Words and expressions hijacked by the demented
can only be said again with their intonation.
Consequently I try - in this place of sagging skin,
of deflated old age - to not take anything in
for every one of the working day's eight hours.

Numinous as this old man's fears might once have been he has
forgotten now why he is frightened. Daily the damaged record
of his thoughts gets stuck on a worry within a state of mind from
his mind's past. Those habits of attitude - some still occupying
his brain's worn surface - have today got this old man frightened/
angry over he doesn't know what. So, in amongst the semi-circle
of old women, sat on plastic seats under their knitted blankets and
their stained shawls, he puts up his trembling fists.

Busy with practicalities - who needs feeding,
who changing - I walk around him.

With ferocious incomprehension
the blue eyes blaze out at me
his supposed tormentor.

The comic threatening posture can be changed later by an arm
wrapped around his shoulders. Saying his name loud and friendly-
like I will tell him to come and get something to eat. Relieved at
not having to fight, smiling at this new mate, "No problem," he'll
say; and with the ghost of a swagger he will walk with me to the
dining room. "No problem."

Case Study (8)

Sons grown and left home
her talk is a gabble of worry:
"They're fed up with me.
  Do you think I should..?"
Hers is a subjectivity
so intense
she cannot see a thing
apart from herself,
"I don't know what I..."
When she smokes she takes
small
quick
theatrical puffs,
says she doesn't know why
she is smoking,
rubs the cigarette out
with short rapid jabs.
"Now I don't know what
  to do with myself..."

In a time of elm's green unfurlings
an overnight storm causes the deaths
of eleven people.
Upon this being reported to her
she says
"I know.
 Wind kept me awake all night.
 Sleeping tablets don't work.
 Do you think I should..?"

Is This The Way?

In foyer and smoking room
sat on low green chairs
are people who have disappeared

so deep inside themselves
that now their external presence
is also not seen.

In the centre of the foyer
stand two professional men
talking softly belly to belly

as if in private. In private
one of these men has safely
confessed his sexual shames

and his petty spites
to the demented. "That'll cook
your goose," one responded.

Another, wandering, tried
the office door, then its window,
"Is this the way?"

You First

Asylum legend - tales of both staff
and patients - leads to this grouping
one end of a corridor, waiting
for someone to kick off. "He's about
to blow," they keep saying, "He's about
to blow." Those nurses, who have so
obviously never fought (at school
they were probably the sunken-chested
sniggerers, or those who laughed
with the teachers at the fools),
are now twitching with glee
at the thought of becoming involved
in a safe fracas (we always,
but always, outnumber the patient)
and can't wait until after to tell
of their part in it. Given the nod,
now, they approach the action with
a gunfighter's finger flex. But rarely
rarely at the front.

Government & Being

If instinct is nature's intellect then human intellect is the recognition
of cause and consequence, with theories built upon expectations, and
- proven - the imposition of patterns. The more complex a pattern
discerned, or invented, the more its veracity becomes a matter of faith.
Wanting to have a faith is like wanting to be in love - to belong to
another, something other, and thus be made complete, unquestioningly
whole. Like a herd of wildebeest, or a shoal of fry, when stalked they
compact - to lose their vulnerable individuality, to become a more
imposing unity, to confuse by their mass. Not I! Not I! Government
relies on this same fearful faith, on this gathering-together instinct for
self-protection of the governed. Yet all that any government sees is
only its own survival. Killing is a tool of government.

Present & Future

Beyond Here

Beyond here it is the voices of
unknowns become familiars,
or of neighbours, old enemies,
or the muffled plotting of
heads-together children
that day-in day-out bother him.
It is only the neighbours,
though, a constant distraction,
who come in with him: cannot
be heard exactly what they are saying,
but he can hear them outside
every door here, mumbling
beyond every of the four
walls, deriding him in
whispers at the end of
every corridor, lying on
the floor of every ceiling
to wheezing-wheezing laugh at him;
or to tut.
Cameras in keyholes, in
ceiling corners, microphones
buried in the plaster of walls
record his dismissive
gestures, his defiant
mutterings. Beds extract
his resentful thoughts.
All wires are aerials,
radiators double as receiving grills.
They know. They know.
Won't let him go.

Today, Yesterday, The Day Before

In this closed brick building, over-heated, under-ventilated,
all is different, extreme. To simplify here, therefore,
is the object, self-administered nicotine
adding to the prescribed sedation, smoke staining yellow along
the tiled ceilings. Carpets are mottled flame-resistant,
the furniture fag-scarred. Here,
among already deconstructed people, any analogy
is dangerous. Here,
where dreamt pain feels real, is manifested
in a tremulous anxiety, pale sweats, a rocking,
any metaphor can only add to the confusion. Here,
where the admitting behaviours were out there labelled mad
- because to have done that they had had to be mad -
mad is what it is called and surreal is what
continues to happen (the stupid, in particular, do so
enjoy being dramatic); and here,
where all relationships are fraught with betrayals,
and patients and staff alike are faced by
the smiling patience of the incumbent psychopath; here
any literary artifice has to be an over-icing. (Familiars

know that madness is not
to be safely imagined, psychoses replicated
by a rattle of nouns, flicker of images, nor by
associative free-flow assumptions, nor by
the portrayal of an obsessive interest
in spider-spinning minutiae. Nor can depression,
say, be conveyed in turgid strung
out slow-mo. Such creative depictions
have other agendas: madness is an experience
best externally observed. Sufficient to note
that its sufferers, more obviously than most,
inhabit worlds of their own creation.)
Shared sounds, coming from other rooms, are of nurse and
doctor chatter, phones ringing and beeping, telly jingles,
earpiece tap-tap and buzz, crack and whisper of fireproof doors
opening, bump of their closing. Old magazines
are read, cups of tea are made. Out the back,
beyond the reinforced glass door, a grey wind
is blowing white plastic chairs along the strip of garden.

Kevin Carter.
*(Photographer born 1960,
killed himself 1994)*

You didn't give it time.

You wept for four hours
after the vulture crouched over
the skin and bone Ethiopian.

You didn't give it time.

The morning after Oosterbroek's death
you were back in Thokoza.

You didn't give it time.

Given time these crazy images
(what price? who pays?
 what connections? - Fame...)
would not have belonged to you.

Still wouldn't have made sense;
but, given time,
(we all of us exploit, are exploited)
they'd have weighed less.

Polemic - in the shape of a poem
because we have been conditioned by poetry
to treasure the English countryside
- poetry being a weapon of rebellion
and the countryside having always
been under threat from those
who claim to own it.
Been etched upon our collective psyche
therefore
appealing images of gnarled trees
standing anciently alone
in dappled pastures; and conjunctions
of ragged hedgerows, cross-hatchings
of fields...
all made icons.
But
when you come to look at what
you have been trained to love
- shape of woman, lie of land -
and you know the one is
silicon synthetic, at best cosmetic,
and the other poison-sprayed, then
pleasure dies in the eyes.

Beside glowing upland lakes of yellow rape
fields of blue flax reflect squares
of powdered sky; and cloud shadows
go flying on over sterile oblongs
of young corn and darken
the black glistening field spawn of
plastic-wrapped silage.
Love this.

Incident 2

Every recent handover, bar the hurried one that begins his nightshift - 32 patients to be told of in 30 minutes - when previously they had mentioned the patient - he who haunts the corridors - they had said to be careful: when he gets into this state - face masked, staring - he will, without warning, lash out at any passing member of staff. The patient is ex-army. The nightshift nursing assistant - in his waking fog of night/days, and used anyway to stepping around the patient as if he isn't there - takes the first punch full on the cheek.

Incident 3

[Speaking as they find salt-of-the-earth nurses will colloquially praise some patients and, with curses, condemn others. Staff are only human, apologists will say; and, of course, they cannot help but respond to people as people. Albeit that those same nurses will then demand to be treated as professionals.]

With extreme diffidence
this middle-class lady,
tweedy and anxious,
approaches the duty nurse
to ask a simple question
about her pills, or going home
on leave, an uncertainty, nothing more.
Yet the plump nurse turns on her
a face sour as a green apple and

snaps at her to make up her mind what it is
she wants to ask and until then not to bother her
                    Staggering backwards
        the patient reels around a corner
        pale and speechless with shock,
        gagging on tears, a feeble hand
        pushing away concern.
                    This reaction, observed,
        is reported to the duty nurse,
        in her tasselled skirt,
        who dismisses it as hysteria.
                    This patient, however,
        has not acted like this before;
        and the next day she is found
        trying to hang herself. Her self-esteem
        was known to be low, but
        she hadn't done that before
        either. Although this same nurse
        has often shouted at other patients
        and subordinates, and continues
        to think highly of herself.

*[In psychiatry, and psychotherapy, any action can be justified
by any outcome, the protagonist claiming - after the event - that
that is exactly what was intended.]*

What Is Social, What Mental Illness?

Take M. He likes a drink. But it fuddles him. His flat becomes a mess, he loses the time of day, the electricity and phone don't get paid, court applications are made; and his money starts to get taken off him at source, leaving him with not enough even for a drink. With the circle of debt starting to tighten M takes himself to the police station. He tells the officer behind the desk that he has a voice in his head telling him to slit the gizzards of young children. As before the police call the on-duty psychiatrist. As before, being new and not knowing M, and most certainly not wanting to take the risk of M slitting a child's gizzard (a sharpened knife, as before, was found on M), the on-call psychiatrist diagnoses alcoholic dementia and M is taken by ambulance to hospital.

In hospital M is encouraged to a bath and is put on a librium detox, usual duration a week. M doesn't get better within the week. Tremors and sweats over, he develops other symptoms, becomes incontinent of faeces and talks still of the voice. Puzzled, his new consultant won't take the risk, yet, of discharging him home. In the fourth week of his stay M says that he is starting to feel better. (Timing is everything now: after 6 weeks in hospital his disability allowance will get drastically cut, is a headache to get reinstated.) After 5 weeks in hospital, the voice gone, the consultant feels safe enough to allow M home - on new medication, to his flat cleaned by Social Services. With his accumulated back pay M clears off the last of the bills, treats himself to a drink, buys a new knife, sharpens it.

Dialogue 49
Inward-looking Modernism

> The world has languages inadequate
> to our changing circumstances,
> to our new situations,
> our new emotions.
> Every generation has to re-invent language,
> to rescue it from an establishment
> that will have assimilated, and nullified,
> the preceding generation's words of self-assertion.
> Language is philosophy,
> is of itself ideology.
> Any totalitarian state will have applied
> new expressions of approbation
> to its leading functionaries.
> Capitalism will have hijacked similar expressions
> as marketing tools.
> Self is language, is a concept
> that cannot exist without language.
> Far too many essays now are preoccupied with
> social alienation, their authors boasting
> a facile view of themselves as
> 'Exiles in their own countries'.
> Writers are the principal re-inventors.
> Yet they are essentially optimists
> self-pressed into pessimistic roles.
> Thus are their messages never clear.
> Such is the price of wanting to be,
> of making their own selves, different.
> Real estrangement has more to do
> with a sense of falsity
> a false world forcing the self
> to be false.
> By the very act of writing,
> of having to use inadequate language,
> writers therefore qualify.

Family As Victim

She says
"For once in my life
 I'm going to be selfish."
This from
a fat and fussy eater.
"Yes, for once in my life,"
she says with the confiding chuckle
of everyone's gran,
"I'm going to do just
 what I want to do."

This overweight woman has always done just
what she wants to do, is saying this now
only because her display
of conventional unselfishness
"...things I've done for you..."
didn't get the result she wanted.

She will feign illness this one,
attempt suicide (overdoses
of limited duration),
and talk much of love and responsibility,
her happiness and unhappiness,
in the training of her family.
They blame themselves.

Jangled

"Wasn't me,
  was the ghost in me
  made me do
  those things."

Hiccups in internal communication,
thought processes impaired:
a mind unhinged is unable
to close itself
to unwanted thoughts.

"The ghost in the machine
  messes up the works."

Whether it's labelled disassociation
or flight-of-ideas
all can still unify
to make a sort-of rationale.

"On the street
  I feel the eyes
  peeling skin from me
  layer by layer."

Addicts All

(1)
Heroin-thin he does the junky float,
eyes marble white, face drawn to a point,
the passing-by glide single-minded
- to score, or, to steal to score
>   (A whole world of needs and musts is balanced in his brain
>   - hence he keeps his head on the same plane as he walks. Needle-
>   sharp his isolation, as tiny as his pupils. Sight is inward.)
Vocabulary, when he does speak,
is vaguely liberal - all the freedoms
for himself. Yet he despairs of himself,
seeks no answer in himself,
wants some other
- a charitable programme, detox clinic -
to take responsibility for his becoming free.
Some other he can blame for his failure.

Dependence increases passivity.

(2)
Puppet-master of her legs the alcoholic throws them
twitching forward in a parody of a walk,
struggling always uphill
against a gale, telling herself,
for every of life's minor adversities,
a drink is what she needs.
>   (Thought here, though superficially societal, is only
>   of suffused self. No give and take to any relationship; only what
>   others can do, have done, to her. She'll flop
>   over anyone for a drink, while drunk, curses
>   all who've used her.)
Self-esteem is so low, brain-cells so damaged,
she's forgotten most of her shames, gets sent
for de-tox only when her relatives, or neighbours,
or social services, can't cope.

On the unit she sits with other alcoholics, who tell stories to make each other laugh in a mimic good time, scoff at the dull and sober world, boast of amounts drunk; and so she talks herself into an early discharge. Back out remembered bravado gets her quickly stewed. Waking cold, having pissed the bed, she despises herself.

Dependence increases passivity.

Dialogue 19
1% Carbon Monoxide Kills

Novelists and torturers know
that cherished habits and routines
are easily, readily broken, abandoned,
that people will accommodate to
whatever's unavoidable.
> Attach cruelty to a system of logic
> and the amount of pain
> one human being can inflict
> on another is infinite.
On alternate days
everyone can be
Herr Eichmann
and Mother Theresa.
> What is most frightening is
> there are actually people,
> real people,
> who prey on kindness
> spongers, con-men, petty thieves.
Trouble with heroes
is they all get themselves
killed in the end.

Strictly Hierarchical

A consultant (god) is not to be argued with. Not, leastways, by nurses (angels). Nor are nurses allowed to openly defy even those house doctors, their placements always temporary, who affect a working cynicism in the hope that it will be mistaken for inside-out knowledge. And while consultants may actually say, have said, pulling rank, "Here I am God"; apart from their salaries, disproportionate to their input (all work from manuals), most consultants earn only the contempt of nurses. Burnt-out on-duty consultants diagnose over the telephone, prescribe for patients they have never known. Or, of late frightened of the immediacy of the mad, after the briefest encounter (and perversely ignoring the recommendations of the nurses who have 24 hour contact, as if to prove themselves still capable of taking charge) this overpaid suit will write up medication designed solely to keep the patient quiet. Or another consultant may have become so completely afraid of taking risks that he, knowing that most psychiatry consists of hit-and-miss diagnoses, will keep his patients so long in hospital that they will develop illnesses they never had before. Or the consultant himself becomes obsessive, ascribes all and every symptom to this month's theory - usually 'merely behavioural' due to a 'personality disorder'. Which diagnoses, again, allows the consultant to do nothing. Or he/she prescribes the drug of the month (came with free mugs, free pens, a video and a 3 course lunch).

None of the above incompetencies will see any consultant sacked. Rather they will be quickly passed on with fulsome references. (Nurse grapevines, however, will ensure that their real reputations and nicknames go with them.) If old enough, of course, crap consultants will be retired early; can then take with them a glowing self-esteem and tales of 'in my day...' For the nurses this new day, this next day, this patient is here, now.

Cringe

On days when the patients are all
in their rooms, or are sat in groups
 in the smoking and TV lounges,
when the qualified staff are gathered in
the office, when the untrained assistants
are in the tea room and the domestics
are having a fag, then the patient who
comes to ask a question asked before
will be condescended to by a fat thicko
younger than her daughter but who
once happened to undergo three years
painful training, which means she was
coaxed and coached through her every exam;
or this worried patient will be shouted at
by an untrained nursing assistant who
just needed a job and this had seemed
like an easy number.
From all ranks
of this 'caring profession'
come the everyday uncouth
who shout across conversations, who bark
an irritated response to a polite request,
who barge into others' privacy, intrude into
others' thoughts; who look through, talk through,
who dismiss the human being standing
in this place
before them; who brush past, walk around,
talk around as if not there...

Illness?

The problem, if it is perceived as a problem,

> socially unacceptable symptoms
> versus
> socially acceptable symptoms

can lie not so much in the affliction
> (there is no cure)
but (where medication leads more to
symptom displacement than cure)
in how   one   copes with it.   Because   such 'cures'
can cause   as many problems as   the 'illness'.
Professionals   accept this: the side-effects   being   the
price of   the 'cure'   even if   the cure   is only temporary
and   the side-effects   permanent.   For instance
Procyclidine is given   for the parkinsonian
side-effects   caused by   most   anti-psychotic
medications.   One side-effect   of Procyclidine,
however,   is to slow   the patient's   reactions.   Between
question   and answer   are long   pauses.
Staff can,   or not have time   to wait,   appear   impatient
and   terminate   conversations   before they are   complete.
Or   the staff   grow tired   of the patients' same old
same old complaints.   This impatience   being   in part
caused by   their own   inability   to counter
the side-effects   again   complained of

All Is Light, Light!

We, this group in attendance,
                are all in slow motion.
While he,
a college kid in drug-induced psychosis,
picks up a cleaner's word
said two doors away,
repeats and enlarges upon it, while we...

we have just become aware that
                it's been said.

Prepared to be amused, one of us
will always pay attention to this spill of words,
catchphrases mostly, associative tracks, but we
can be startled (truths said in psychosis are no less
truths because they are said in psychosis).
He, meanwhile,
has seen significance in the shape
                of a stain
                on the wall, has
 invented a superstition, lain a penny
                face out
on the sink edge, now walks
the carpet line along the door...

        At a signal (eyebrows raised, a nod)
we move in close. One of us starts to explain
the need for an injection. He protests,
goes to resist. But, quick as he is,
we are too many and we know
                what has to be done.

Instant History

Again, born again,
I will step out of my mouth and

from the fire-spark of my becoming, throughout
the tinder-race of the new years,

a globe of water sizzling to extinction
on the tongue's hot-plate, within

the soot-oven of the mouth, deafened
and comforted by the not-yet

not-yet beat of the throat's heart, I will
be again my eternity's one true candle.

Short Term Measures / Life Sentences

You think you've got off the charge,
out of the mess, by claiming mental illness.
But, for mental illness to be mental illness,
it must, perforce, be treatable. And treatable
means medication. And any medication means
side-effects. Side-effects mean more,
mean different, medications. (And, by now,
every single little thing you say of what
you think will be taken as symptomatic
of your mental state.) Your care plan
will be amended, medication altered
accordingly... Your life sentence began
back when you claimed, in mitigation,
mental duress.

Case Study (9)

Newcomers can find themselves wanting the round blue eyes
and the sorrowful expression
to be innocent of premeditation. Sit with her an hour
or so though
and one becomes aware that she doesn't so much
ignore the tv's news
of this and that disaster
- to avoid adding the world's new troubles,
  like a depressive,
  to the weight of her own crippling despair -
rather she is dismissive of such calamities
because
they don't involve her.

Of all the odd comings and goings here
she walks past the violently acting out
and those besmirched
in a mess of anxiety,
selecting only those incidents
which she can use
to attack her accusers. (Observing, one soon suspects
  that the incarcerating act was born
  not out of desperation, but was an interrupted
  step-by-step calculation; that even
  her being here, in this place, is her building
  of a case, her working up a plea.)
One sees the round blue eyes sadly assess the next
newcomer come to assess her;
and one notes the wise, after an hour, leave
carrying a new hope now
that they don't figure in her plans.

Circles

A circle is allegedly democratic. Sat in a circle we are all supposedly equal. The circular chaos of some people's lives, however, has them end up always in the same kind of relationships, same kind of debts, will find them standing again in the middle and gazing inwards at the mess... Often all that is required to bring order to such a muddled life is that a decision is made, a tangent drawn. What is decided, which course is chosen, is not in itself important, only that a decision is made. And the psychiatrist it is who has to make that decision, to show that there is a route out of such debilitating distress. First the restorative powers of sleep, then do this, and this, then this. There are no sides to be taken, policies enacted, only an outcome to be sought. So can no psychiatrist seek popularity; nor, at the top of his tree, can there be any buck-passing, no putting off, no anything-for-a-quiet-life. What he says - leave your abusive partner, sell your too-large house, pack in your too-demanding job - will not be what his patients want to hear. They may cry, but will try to stop their tears, because they will have been given these instructions in the crowded room of the weekly ward round. Doctors, nurses, social workers, trainees, will have seated themselves in a circle, the better to look into this crowded mind. And these professionals too are imperfect people, omissions in their training compounded by traits in their personalities. Here the hard-faced nurse whose every sigh is a value judgement. Here the junior doctor who makes of everything said a joke. Here a trainee who seems only to giggle about her new clothes. Here the always late Social Worker looking at her bleep. A stranger, when she entered this already seated circle; a stranger, being here in this building all the time, to their seven-and-a-half hour world; a stranger to the psychiatric mind-set (a gestalt which closes itself into its own world, own terms of reference); the patient looks around at them all and doesn't take in a word.

Insight, *n. power of seeing into and understanding things;*
imaginative penetration: practical knowledge: enlightenment:
a view into anything.
Insight, *n. (Scot,) household goods, furniture*

Suppose insight is the ability to step outside yourself
        and look back in. But what if,
tomorrow, you started having what others describe as
        auditory hallucinations;
would you, those unattached voices being undeniably present,
        would you promptly believe in
a spirit world, give credence to all kinds of supernatural
        phenomena; or would you, yesterday rational,
be inclined towards the proffered physical/mechanical
        explanation of slower synapses
being overtaken by the same message and your mind thus
        misinterpreting the second?
Suppose insight is living in a house but with the radio
        and the tv tuned to foreign stations.
Without going out of doors you will not know where you are.
        To step outside, however, will require
doubt of your situation; and a personality that is unable
        to think itself fallible must go
along with its mind's misinformation, will reply or respond to these
        new part-heard voices. If intelligent,
and contemptuous of practical causes offered up by those
        patently not so clever or as well-read,
then this mind will construct elaborate alternatives,
        delusional edifices and value systems.
Chairs may get stacked in the centre of a room, ovens get used
        as altars, tables cooked upon, beds slept
under; anything other than admit to the possibility
        of your own mind misleading itself.

Happy Ever After

Thought she'd won
when she found herself
married with kids.

But now all there is
is this
marriage and kids.

All Power Is Abusive

Small power now   in any household   is a puzzle
to be wrinkled out   by picking up   on   in public
hesitant deferences   and subtle   compliances.
John Clare, though,   lived when power   was naked
and a man could be   addressed as   'Master'
as a statement of fact.   John Clare was not
master of himself.   Displaced   from not only
his home   and environs   but, by his poetic success,
from his class too   he knew   that he had no control
over any of the life   about him.   An unsealed half
- his twin sister   Besse   had died at birth -
he was raw   to every affront   against the natural.
Enclosure's destruction   of an ancient ivy-grown stile
made him   sick-to-the-pit-of-his-stomach.   But
where to escape?   The instinct   of every frightened animal
is to stay still   and hope   that their   immobility
will hide them.   Thus   do domestic bullies
come by their power: their victims,   afraid of moving,
hammered into place   absorbing   every new violation.

A Passive Woman

A passive woman
she soaked up men's affections
until there was only anger left.
The men, despising themselves
for their anger, left her.

He found her. Now
this old man's every move
is calculated aggression
- a slam
  snatch
  clutch
  snap

A passive woman
she seems to have grown a capacity
for hurt too.
While his has become the kind of anger
we have at ill people, at ill pets,
who, despite all our best efforts,
won't get better.
Even the skinny sight of them
(of her anticipating fresh hurt)
can make us angry.
(And Home is where we can
  indulge our smallest irritation.)

A passive woman
she, eyelid flicker of a wince,
waits.

Museum Piece

Like so many women her age
she was initially undone
by being drawn to danger,
to that masculine sense
of suppressed menace.
(A craving on her part for passion,
 for excitement?) A razor's edge she,
of course, couldn't blunt.
Began with his practising
hurtful things to say. And still
she stayed, even when the anger
(suffused, frustrated
- warrior without a war)
 punched out at her.

Surviving into another day
she comes here - to this still room,
among these glass cases, in which
bits of the past are positioned for worship,
and squeak-shoed visitors
talk in polite whispers -
to sit on a hard bench
and close herself to herself.

Straight-backed,
one hand takes the other
and places it in her lap.

Her bruises are ignored.

Nurse

In the name of a later, greater good
you learn to accept.

You learn to accept that patients are occasionally
caused pain by your actions.

Caused pain by your actions, your ministrations
in the name of a later, greater good.

(You, heretic, intimate of death,
  know that not all sick people
  can be made well. You,
  bully of the ill,
  hide this unease
  behind the blatant candour
  of your eye contact.)

Loss

Like an ankle-snared fox
biting off his own leg
so do the divorcing have to
kill parts of themselves
to be free. Photographs
    that were once a catechism
    of safe remembering are
    with news brought
    from this new past,
    with the tiniest
    of old secrets exposed (as if
    she, as if he, already knew)
    - are all seen now as lies.
    Every camera-recorded smile
    is duplicitous, every group
    arrangement indicative
    of betrayals imminent.
Hobbling towards another tomorrow
they meet everyone and everything,
even and especially their own feelings,
with a cringing away distrust.

6:23am

We clocks extrapolate this one minute's heartbeat
to a lifetime's expectancy. We clocks know that
each girl will come to an age
when she will fill her skin to bursting
like a golden plum. We clocks know too
that she will thicken into motherhood.
Thereafter the girl she once was will shrink
slowly inside her loosened skin.
Stray moments of that life can be assassinated
with a camera. Another method
of halting Time's asymmetrical flow
is to write it down. The time is now 6:23am.
6:23am on this page for as long as
this page may last. Forever?
Fools no-one. Except the writer who wants
to be fooled. Other artefacts can accidentally be
where memories get stored; to each thing a history,
utensils opening like books. Sportsmen actually
want to be a statistic. Of the past. A gardener,
on the other hand, looks always, not
at what a plant is but at what it will become.
In the Here and Now
punctuality can become a disease,
an affliction which will have the organised
driving through sparkling green countryside
down a tunnel of worry - I'm late! I'm late!
      (They will also have to crowd in
        the hiatus times of holidays.)
In the present the clock of loneliness
is a thin red fish circling in a waterglobe.
There are no victims. We it is
who choose to measure time's passing.

Poor Self-Esteem

All our lives
we've been sold
crap food
crap clothes
crap cars
crap houses
crap dreams

Identifying with the struggle, I know
how near the edge I am. But
I'm nowhere near as close as you
who are walking backwards towards it.

> Talking therapies
> have the onion self
> peeled apart.

> It stinks.

One In Six

One in six people you will, at some time in your life, suffer a mental illness. When the world's failings are visited upon you what you will need, above all else, is a philosophy. Do not expect a cure. Cure implies being able to achieve a permanent and perfect state of health, of existence. Which is self-evidently impossible. Any 'cure' on offer, therefore, and its concomitant treatment, because impermanent, because permanently incomplete, must perforce become a part of your illness. A few of you will be wise enough to blame the 'cure'. Most of you though, being unable to achieve, or to maintain, a perfect state of existence, you will come to regard yourselves as intrinsically imperfect, yourselves at fault, yourselves to blame.

The life-philosophies that are available to most people are contained within a religious framework. Now a harassed priest might tell you that religion is prone to the mentally ill, not the mentally ill to religion; but most religions promote 'cures' for life's ills. Siddhartha G offered 'cures', as did Christ. Diagnosed ill, you have been changed. But 'ill' you may have been misnamed. Because there never was any returning to perfect health: medication was therefore not a promise to be believed. And even more so the vaguer promises of religion - with their uncertain sense that seems to accommodate your disordered thoughts, that can seem to understand your puzzled want. You will, though, become ever more frustrated, distraught, by religion's pedantic lack of specifics. There will come a time when, only in medicated euphoria, you will still believe yourself able to believe.

A Type/A Category

     Letter reversals and
distractive behaviours unrecognised (or, more likely,
remedial teaching then, as now, underfunded)
he slipped ever behind.
     Clumsy, awkward, feeling mocked, scoffed at
he skipped school. Come sixteen, illiterate, he tried
to enter a world of form-filling and signposts. An immediate
failure, he found himself in the street company
of other outcasts.
     The emulation of their odd antics
(a normative response, but over-proving himself)
had him arrested and, further acting out (a dumbshow fear
of paper, an ape-like grunting at printed matter)
had him labelled mentally ill.
     On admission he displays an obsessive
(ironical?) reverence for books, walks holding one before him
open at a middle page. The cups of tea in his other hand
get slopping spilt.
     This dyspraxia is acknowledged; but that
does not lie under the psychiatrist's remit. So
this young man, unable to expand his thoughts without
benefit of paper, of cross-referenced constructs, and
with few alternative models, other than telly,
to draw from.
     his powers of expression curtailed (he cannot
explain himself to himself), his insight into his condition
as narrow as that of the specialists prescribing for him,
he is offered counselling for his anger, medication
for his anxiety.

Stoppeth

Violations get stoppered. Who to tell when no other has had this done to them? Or those that have, or so it is half-rumoured, they are weak and despised, and who, in their right mind, is going to admit to being like them? So, untold, again and again, it gets done to them, the self betrayed each time, and with each betrayal choked down. Simple laws of physics say that such compression in such a singular space must reach a point where the process gets reversed. Happens in an instant. Begins with an animal bellow, a rocking cry. And, once begun, this bottled talk, one-sided, fragmentary, pressure to tell not allowing a steady flow, metaphysical assertions mixed with outrageous histories, the talk itself becomes a disputed record, another shameful fact to not be denied - in what has been said is a fact, but it is not the truth. The truth is somewhere deeper, behind, further down, not yet here and bursting to be told.

Second Thoughts

The sympathetic, who work with abuse cases, in their self-recognition of the symptoms, can come to believe that they too might have been abused, the memory buried. The sympathetic who work with the mentally ill, in their self-recognition of the symptoms, can come to believe that they are about to become mentally ill. In this profession the sympathetic - in the technical sense, resonating to the same vibrations - are further handicapped by their disinclination to interfere. When telling others how to behave they see themselves distastefully as bullies, worry at their fallible influence, that they - damaged goods themselves - should be so presumptuous as to shape another's life? Yet they will be the first to concede that some people can be, for their own sake, ought to be, bullied into getting better. Which is how the very act of nursing brutalises. Aside from sheer numbers. Bodies come, faces complain; patients get repaired, or die, go anyway. Only the odd, the unusual, only those become stories get remembered. The rest pass through. Leaving the sympathetic - at a loss to recall the face, the name - to question the value of what they do.

Next To

If the bathroom was the first or
was the most frequent place of abuse
that child can come to see dirt as
an expression of purity renewed.

Wallowing in a bacterial slime of
old sweat and unwashed underthings,
slinking by in the safe-making stink
of sockless trainers, with her scissor-cropped

hair matted, teeth unbrushed, this
twelve-year-old can feel protected from
the impulse she knows too well wants
- above all else - to violate innocence.

And for innocence read purity;
and for purity - where all are taught
to get ourselves and our houses sparkling
like on the adverts - read cleanliness.

A pair of female workers in a children's home
will Mutt-and-Jeff shame and encourage
her towards a shower, will introduce her
to fashion pages, cosmetics and perfumes.

Both will count her becoming clean and
wearing lip-stick a personal success. But at
every one of her future life's crises she will
seek sanctuary in 'self-neglect', in 'lack

of personal hygiene'. And again, and again
someone in the caring professions will cap
a story with how dirty she was, will
declare her 'better' when clean.

Dialogue 29
Family Damage

Abnormality does not bring happiness.
Deliberately acting other than normal
can occasionally bring satisfaction,
rarely happiness.
All through their lives the abused think
Now I can confess what was done to me.
And they don't.
There has always to be the suspicion
that when the pressures get too much
some seek refuge in psychosis,
take a holiday from life's decisions.
I despise those who use their psychosis
as a licence to inflict hurt.
Forsaking all responsibility
they laugh at windows,
utter whatever jangled nonsense
enters their mouth. Cynics us
can see through their ploys, may itch
to slap them back to normality.
But oh
what a place to seek sanctuary.
How bleak are our lives.
As bleak as the sea.
As bleak as the countryside.
colossal
unappeasable loneliness.
We live in a time when only
the sufferings of those deemed mad
make any kind of sense.

We Should All Be Born Orphans, Then Sterilised

The worse realisation is that
they don't mean anything by it, not to you;
they just take what's there for the taking. But
they fuck you up fucking you your Mum & Dad.
You soon learn not to get in the way of them;
because the fucking's only the half of it: your needs
can only interfere with their wants. Dogs
are treated better in your house: you're just there
to get screamed at   to clean up the mess,
a fucking nuisance. Until she's bored and
she wants you to go down on her, or
he's feeling especially bitter this day and decides
to fuck you up the bum. Telling you, of course,
that it's all your fault. And it never occurs to you,
the child, that they, the abusers, want
to keep it secret. So ashamed are you, outside
or in school, you're afraid that they're the ones
who'll tell. We should, all of us, be born orphans.

Yea Yea

Cause is boredom, born out of familiarity;
the daily dealing with the ill and complaining,
the put-on doleful face and wasp-in-a-jar whine.
Being visibly unmoved can make even the most
caring nurse seem cynical. Take, for instance,
a pit nurse - she gets to sneer at miners who
come to her worrying they may have got silicosis:
yea yea, she thinks, she being their first call
on the road to compensation. While a psychi nurse
gets to hear so many stories of abuse, comes to see
each as an excuse to be ill, with the illness
being licence to not take responsibility
for this life they have made their own. Yea yea,
she seems to be saying, of course you were abused,
wasn't everyone?
                    (Apart from her: she wouldn't
have allowed something so unclean, so obscene,
to have happened to her.)
            The patient, meanwhile, has registered
the unmoved face.
            (Removal of trust is one of the consequences
of abuse. Nor can a self so deconstructed
trust itself to be happy.)
            Before, therefore, this inner sneer,
the patient drops his/her head, nape exposed,
becomes yet another psychi victim offering him/herself
up to chance and semantics - which nurse happens to
overhear what, which on-call locum decides upon which
diagnosis, which eeny-meeny-miny-mo medication
to try him/her with this time. The patient
listens to the treatment plan, asks no questions,
knows his/her role. When asked if he/she
understands - wanting only to escape this scrutiny,
this room - yea yea, he/she says.

Not Communication

Seen, heard, thought; whatever its form, sex has an emotive impact. We think, glimpse, acts; we do things, have them thought about us, done to us, do them, which once done we are unable to undo. We take our histories to our every new relationship. Even a whole love, however, cannot benefit from the truth entire. Nor will the amassed experience of the lover, a lifetime's familiarity, be more than one form of knowing. Of part-knowing; because, if any love is to be sustained, there are some truths which cannot be said. (Such truths are mind tumours.) Love/sex, therefore, cannot be communication. Even before that - the long looks into the other's eyes, the hand lingering on the arm, tingle fingers touching shoulder, the belief that you are in the company of a kindred spirit - can be shattered with the first words. Between human beings, where love nor sex is part of the transaction, language is the sole means of unequivocal communication. And then it, for example this, is imperfect.

Dialogue 30
Speak The Unspeakable, Think The Unthinkable

Psychiatry's
is not an illustrious history.
Been on a course
got the vocabulary.
Admit it -
psychiatry is an ongoing experiment,
diagnoses dependent entirely on semantics.
Is always and
ultimately a consensus
of what is acceptable behaviour,
no matter how delusional
the belief that drives it.
We too have been irrationally conditioned.
Below/above
what level of mental competence
are we judged? By whom?

Suspicion

The little fat girl says that she saw a strange man at the school gates, tries to get her best friend to say that she saw him too. Her friend tells the police that her friend said that she saw the man leave in a silver car. No, she didn't see the car. Her friend saw the silver car.

The little fat girl says that the dark-haired girl, who her mother minds after school, told her to put a grey knitting needle into her vagina. The dark-haired girl stamps her foot, puts her hands to her hips; and she sulks because she thinks her busy mother doesn't believe her.

The little fat girl says that the new teacher took out his penis and asked her to touch it. She says that he whispered to her that the devil would get her if she told.

The little fat girl's mother, beside herself, won't let her daughter be interviewed by the police without her being there, keeps her daughter home from school.

The teacher, although he is told that his protestations of innocence are believed by the police and by all the school governors, stays on a year, then leaves.

The Good Nurse

The good nurse adjusts her body clock
to synchronise with each
                    rotational shift.
The good nurse reads
what others have left for her to read.
The good nurse
pauses
before she speaks.
The good nurse makes time, takes
her time, elicits from the patient more
than that patient intended
                    to disclose.
The good nurse leads the house doctor
to the diagnosis as if it was his/
                    as if it were her/ own idea
(knowing that any transparent presumption
 will antagonise him/her into proving
 this underling wrong).
                    Ditto medication.
The good nurse uses herself
                    in therapeutic roles,
                    breaks all the rules
she thinks it necessary to break;
and records the salient facts to cover her back.
The good nurse out-schemes the manipulative
personality, takes the caring but
                    not-too-bright assistant
to one side to quietly tell him/her
not to pander to the manipulator's demands;
takes them aside
                    to quietly tell them again.
The good nurse traps the consultant into
signing irksome papers (but which will allow
 the patient some due freedom), before
the consultant goes off for the weekend.

The good nurse seeks to see things from
her patient's point of view; and seeks to
change the way of seeing that is proving
so harmful to said patient.
The good nurse is properly sceptical, does not
believe her managers or the politicians;
the good nurse knows that
with more resources she could provide
the service the patients deserve.
The good nurse, conscience consulted,
is looking for another job.

Saints Aplenty

Those, once, who mortified their own flesh,
who beat and cut and starved themselves,
if also holy-minded, oft came to be canonised.
Now we label it self-harm and religious mania
and offer up 'cures'.

Abuse disperses the self to the surface.
Vacuum is filled by a guilt, creates
an upside-down inside-out logic
which seeks, not relief from, but
- to exorcise, at best distract -
the mental hurt, replace it with a physical.

But - it not working, the accusing voice
still there - having sliced into
the tops of his legs, he increases the pain
by slowly pouring bleach into each
of the mouth-like wounds and, head back, he
holds onto the throb and gnaw like his breath.

I Think I Think

I work where words are often not/
      a currency of exchange
but are symptomatic of states/
      the manner of their use
denoting certain conditions:/
      pressure of speech (tho' better called
speed-speaking); or the/
      staring down significance attached to
(apparently) random words uttered/
      by the psychotic; or the verbal salads
of the internally/
      disconnected; or the echolalia
of the mind-blown. And one still,/
      occasionally, comes upon
the compulsive la-la rhyming/
      in the diminution of dementia.
After seven-and-a-half hours a day/
      on the receiving end of this
I go voluntarily to sit/
      on hard chairs in a scattering of audience
and listen to pause-ridden/
      allusive verses
delivered in soft voices,/
      and weighted with various symbolisms
that require long and/
      arcane explanations; or I listen to
the stutterings and glottal/
      rumblings of deconstructionist
'L=anguage' poets in pursuit of/
      associative tracks; or
even to determined rhymesters/
      banging on, and on...
And I think.../
      I think, "They're all mad."

Poets Must Be Seditious, Or They Lie

Here in this written reality
we are not censored,
do not have to write in code.
The majority though
continue to lie about sex.
Offended by expected rejection
matriarchies still make
of male homosexuality
a crime,
force men into templates
contrary to their true natures.
Which is not only the slap of leather and brutality,
but also the wifely knowledge that
having someone to care for
gives the same contentment as
being cared for by someone else.

A digression: our real fear here,
poets,
is of seeming too straightforward,
of having, transparently, nothing to say.

In the empire of this day,
selfishness as ever driving democracy,
worse than censored
we have been sidelined.
The stupid people
- Sun readers and fundamentalists -
are running our world.
Only the loud will be heard.

Case Study (10)

           With a twist of his head
                         away
    he hurries along at a slant,
presents as acutely shy.
Coming to any crowded doorway
he will retreat around the nearest corner,
wait, teetering,
poised
to move his back
quickly past
any warm press of flesh.
           Briefest eye contact,
           he knows
           with the certainty of shame,
           will have all his thoughts
           read.
A slantwise
sideways on world
he knows too that
           his voices live
           in the bevel edge

of mirrors,

that the real TV images

can only be seen

down the sides of the screen.

Yet, a logic has him suspect that, somewhere

there is another sense to be made of these

disparate worlds. So

 he listens attentively to the inner

                              the outer

                    and the ones behind.

Humour

     is the product of any logic

                         upended:

his laughter (said, in his notes,

                 to be 'inappropriate'

                 no matter whence its stimulus)

has to be a considered

and therefore

mechanical response.

It will be terminated

          with a glance.

Jelly Grown-Ups

Dreams - personal, public and political -
outlive their time. I'm sceptical now
of all those who,   in dress or deed,
would be heroes: the clear jelly
of their time will hold them - amusing
specimens.   I, though, despise
this cynicism in myself: it adds to the smell
of adult defeat. Yet   neither can I, being of this
time, not participate in it
at the age that I am now   even if a bogus
individuality appears to be the one aim
of any rebellion, apparently for its own sake.
(It is only by such small tokens,
   triumph of a cock-snoop trifle,
   that the middle-aged can raise
   their self-esteem.)   And it's true,
of genius and clowns, that both can, must
have a nose for the absurd. It is to
the young, however, and not those of them
imitating adults,   but the few who
are ranting against the mundane
it is to them that we must look
for idealism in the large.   Not to the old
who have reached accommodations, who
have admitted so many small defeats, who have
stopped struggling,   who are sinking
foolishly into the jelly.

Case Study (11)

This smiling depressive holds onto it all
by her fingernails. Varnished. Red.
She knows what
attracts men. Smiles.
All sex is psychological,
want measuring up to
satisfaction. Natural justice though
doesn't exist: such is her
evangelical certainty.
Smile.
The men she don't want
make advances to her.
Smile, turn away.
The men she finds
she don't want
stay. She keeps
the house clean, herself
tidy. Smiles
at the children,
remembers to ask
about their day. Smiles.
She is an emptiness, takes pills;
but not in the expectation
that they will fill her.
Rather
it is a cancelling
she is after.
  Found,
she smiles.

In Opposite Soft Chairs

As confirmation of their life status
both easily recreate (..the fearful
attract those who want to be frightening)
the circumstances of their earlier
(the making of them) family abuse.

He
openly homosexual now
still seeks approbation from older men
and the choked down
implosive excitement
of violent sex.

She too
continues to play
little surprised girl
to brutal father figures
(not later, bruises masked, forgiving;
 but making no mention).

Come thickening middle age
both are (of a sudden)
too grotesquely old for the role,
have to ask of themself
"Who am I
 aside from victim?"
Can find no self to assert.

Ongoing

Eyes get narrowed over the consideration
that all life's fantasies are founded
on false assumptions.
    Such a thought,
unborn, stays unborn unless given form.
Unexpressed, this thought-foetus,
disintegrating, becomes womb-toxic,
gets re-absorbed into mind's
metabolic processes, will poison,
will occlude, all thought.
    Cogitative process,
    done and undone,
    is unending, a job
    that will not stay
    finished: no-one
    can be cured of this
    life - think now
    what it is
    that is
    trying to be
    explained here.

Mocked By Windows

in orange-grey streets of night
a city's self-creating damp
all cars a street away
         moving slowly
traffic lights undisturbed
red sinking through amber
to green
green rising amber
rising red
wind-dusted pavements belonging to
a labouring drunk
between shift worker
cleaners and the homeless keeping warm
mocked by windows
divisions of glass

No Win

They keep asking me
how I feel,
encourage me
to express my feelings;
and then they
accuse me
of being
self-obsessed.

Mortal Remains

on a hilltop partially walled
closed with eroded hedgerows
          small and made midday dark by dense yews
          weather-screwed
          down ducking paths
worn through untidy floor
of ivy, creeping elder
nettles and feather-seeded grass
          ...equality of death
in this Quaker burial ground
worldly sentimentality nor wealth
          celebrated here
simple principles made
          simple practice
has slabs of stipulated size
stating only name
when born
where lived
when died
          and but few stones
for three centuries of dead
and them awkwardly spread
          unevenly weathered
          despite ironies implied
and wary of the attractive strangeness
          of another faith
I wander from this graveyard
- looking out to drought's yellow fields
  through hillside tall beech and ash
  with a sense of fitness
          full of a peace
from which I've left no other

Frustration upon Frustration

On the cusp between medicine and politics is a profession acting like a science, but with so many variables that it has to - despite its extensive, ever-inventive and all-encompassing terminology - be bogus. For the foreseeable future, however, psychiatry will continue to be the stopgap between the hocus-pocus of faith-healing (unprovable, taken on faith) and a real working knowledge (this pill taken, this happens). Note - faith-healing too blames the victim, cure within themselves; so, should the victim fail to be cured, it has to be their own fault. At its even best psychiatry can only provide the disturbed with a temporary retreat, a sanctuary, can only give them time away from their problems. Medication, alone, can be the retreat, the shut-off sanctuary. But if the victim's circumstances aren't changed - and psychiatry has no power to change them - then the afflicted, victims of their own life, will again take into themselves its sickness.

Politics changes systems, changes societies. Psychiatry, therefore, will only ever be allowed to treat the symptoms, will return its patients, time and again, to the social and familial causes of their illness. Nor is its twin, psychology, allowed to change the causative circumstances, is able only to assist the afflicted towards an eventual coming to terms with the causes of their affliction. The causes, untreated, will remain.

Sisters In Denial

Hoarse
with working class veracity;
Cooing
a middle-class confidence;
No,
not her man screwing around.
No,
not her man abusing her children.
No,
not her man knocking her about.
       Well,
       yes, he did; but
       he didn't mean it,
       things got on top of him.
       I should have...
Bastard!
she says to the new
new friendly ear,
Why should it always be me who..?
You won't
will you...
(So she fails in all her relationships,
  each being an escape from the last.)

Case Study (12)

She cries. Simply that -
her condition, her complaint,
        is what she does - she cries.
Her nose goes red, her eyes swell
        and she cries.
Pitying herself, crying,
        this plain sister,
unable to believe praise
seeks instead to be pitied.
                Crying
                she is, of course,
                single;
                when not here
                lives alone.
Living alone she doesn't bother
        to wash. Even here
she blasts night-breath over
        any who come
        to sympathise.
        Her sister is married,
has her own life to get on with but,
        kind, she makes time,
        brings the children.
Wondering if her sister is ever
        going to get better
she goes seeking out the nurses;
        and in her they confide.
When with her sister, snuffling,
        they try their best
to be patient; but, like today,
        even before her sister and
her quiet polite children have left,
        she is crying again.

Futureless

Huntsmen do enjoy killing (is why they do it).
Developers do bulldoze gardens.
Fields do get sprayed
      with a variety of poisons.
Landlords do evict pregnant women
      (before such women can look pitiful
      with a shawled babe-in-arms).
Governments do cheat the poor.
      You say that all
of the above are beyond your
      personal control;
and you make yourself take notice
instead of the sun's
surface glaze reflection
overlaying the pond's golden carp, you outstare
a little owl squatting in an oak, smile back
at rainbows, recall yourself standing exalted
on mountain's tops. Yet still
visions of walls falling inwards
bring you frightened
out of your dreams.

Observe Minus Medication

If you could sort
the voices you almost hear
into various categories - good, bad,
mischievous, righteous - and construct
a system by which each would find,
eventually, of its own accord, its
allocated space, the voices would become
of no consequence.
If you could saw up
clouds and stack the portions in boxes
skies would become easier to organise.
Although some clouds are bound to escape,
confuse matters, make the cardboard
soggy, the boxes collapse, smudge
the labels.
So now do you go among us
reach-out-and-touch-us
flesh and blood people
as if we are the ghosts
listening for these others

Case Study (13)

                  In his pulpit demeanour,
tobacco hoarse, he says that God
                  Is speaking to him in one voice,
Lucifer in another. He can talk down Lucifer, he says,
                  if left to himself, doesn't,
thank you very much, need our tablets or our injections.

                  Last in a year and a half before
he hasn't been seen for eight weeks, or more;
                  as usual, has been living in
his long black coat and not washing or eating. Crust
                  sits in his lashes, spittle
has dried white in the corners of his mouth, his breath
                  smells of urine and his skin,
through dehydration, is papery thin. God is Light!
                  he rasping declares.
Through God I can see. I see Him!

Unrhymed Couplets

Manic or incompetent, mail order or credit card,
the bills cannot be met out of Disability Allowance.

Anxiety affects the illness. A Social Worker
is appointed intermediary

and the psychiatrist writes a letter
asking for understanding.

Creditors, soon as they hear mental illness, know that
their chances of recovery are marginal, and write off the bill.

The patient's relief is palpable: now they can face
going home, can embrace another new beginning.

(The unpaid-for goods are kept. This way, too,
  the petty crimes get passed over.)

Nurses, overhearing, nurses who had to work nights
because they couldn't afford childminders, or holidays away;

these nurses ask who will pay their bills for them.
And each considers, a moment, the luxury of giving up

this unwinnable struggle, see themselves sat
in a corner crying.

(They've seen more than enough of it
  to know how to act.)

They also see someone, like themselves,
a sneer behind the eyes, looking down on them;

or their children's naked concern, or contempt,
and they know that they won't. So,

with the double burden of dignity and dissatisfaction,
they go on with the job.

Not All Here

with razor-scraped

              lines of white

- doubled on the mirror
  base to apex

              every translucent junky

seeks to make

              a ghost of himself/

herself

              passes by

              prison sly

with that partial smile

              that looks only

how to use

              other people

Remember The Future

Looked at through the lens of your shared humanity
obedience to laws only makes you
appear just: justice, though,
the justice which is not
a biblical pay-back balance,
that justice must live inside us.

Wronged
we can become owned by
destructive truths
that have some satisfaction in the telling
      - Humanity will one day
        succeed in killing itself.
        Maybe not in our lifetime. Deathtime.
        All we can do is listen to ourselves
shout warnings, draw our own attention back to
the small steps being taken now.
Ignored
we, the self-declared innocent,
can say we hope that the crimes of the evil
will return to haunt them.

The evil, however, being evil
do not see their crimes as crimes,
so will give their wrongdoing
not a second thought.

Remember our humanity:
laws only make us appear just.

Justice Is Elsewhere

This big ginger man may have
battered both his wives
into a refuge, may have been

accused of sexual abuse of
his one daughter; but all that
is theoretical, stories from

somewhere else, another time.
Before me now, sunk on the edge
of a hard chair, is a grown man

with his mauve-blotched features
broken open in great blubbing
tears; and, confronted

with such distress, a hand
of its own accord, putting aside
the mind's knowledge, reaches out

to grip
and rock
a shoulder.

Universal Purpose Is Religion's Lie

Good events will follow bad ones
just as bad times will come after
good times. There is
no law to it. Expectation
can possibly influence outcome,
some futures, therefore,
being partly self-made.

I won't be there.

And with hindsight we can, possibly,
see where we have been
and trace, hypothetically, a path
into our futures.

I won't be there.

Hospitalised

What is mental ill-health?
Other than the sickness of society
visited upon the individual?

Hospitals were known, once,
singularly, as places of death,
where people were taken to die.
Now they house our casualties
- RTAs, pollution victims; and those
  who simply can't cope.

Can abnormality be called an illness?
Are poor levels of functioning
an illness? Is hearing voices
only a problem
if it is perceived as a problem?

Psychiatry, this subjective science,
attaches stigmas from a new
expurgatory index and suggests
various treatments.

Those placed here know that
any 'cure' is as phoney as a nurse's smile,
fake as a doctor's certainty.

Point of No Return

Take a girl, any girl,
sports shirt, jeans and ponytail,
who swallows down one small o.d.;
throw away the key.
Take a girl, any girl,
sports shirt, jeans and ponytail,
whose life doesn't measure up
to the sense of her own importance.
                    At a loss
all it takes is one small o.d.
and a nihilistic line in repartee
to begin a career in psychiatry.
Take a girl, any girl,
who wants to excel, to be the best
at something.
Take a consultant, new to the place,
who needs to build a case load.
He tells her,
actually tells her,
what she's thinking.
She, of course, goes one better.
Take a girl, any girl,
sports shirt, jeans and ponytail,
who expresses dangerous ideas
in such a setting.
For her own, and the safety of others,
he detains her under Section 3

of the Mental Health Act, 1983.
Take a girl, any girl,
who's told that she's cleverer
than she is. Intense maybe; but,
her paintings and writings of a type,
she's not got that many GCSEs.
Any psychiatrist, though, is only
as pub-famous as his most
notorious patient, so her talents
are described as 'exceptional'.
Take a girl, any girl,
sports shirt, jeans and ponytail,
who identifies always
with the leader of the pack;
and who, here, has only contempt
for her self-pitying fellow patients.
Take a consultant, just one consultant,
who ignores all and every opinion,
observation and piece of evidence
that stands in the way
of what he wants.
While she, to go that step further along,
has to prove him right/wrong.
                She jumps the fence,
but returns
of her own accord. The game is on.
His counter is to move her
into a semi-secure unit

and give her ECT.
Locked in, with one old
shouting patient, stupidly aggressive,
among junky psychotics, wild and quick,
lived with day and night: it is
the old woman
her frustration
has her attack.
Take a consultant, just one consultant,
who claims this as the violence
that he, from day one, predicted.
And manufactured,
say the many subordinates
who disagree; and, ignored,
mutter their impotence.
To have her promoted to Broadmoor,
however, requires a second opinion.
He goes through three
outside consultants before
he finds one
who will agree
with his diagnosis.
          On the day of her transfer
she weeps.
Take a girl, any girl,
sports shirt, jeans and ponytail,
who swallows down one small o.d.;
throw away the key.